Timeless Lessons for Prayer Warriors.

I0108801

Timeless Lessons for Prayer Warriors

Confirming Kavanaugh
The Spiritual Battle

Zeb Bradford Long

PRMI
EXOUSIA
PRESS

PRMI EXOUSIA PRESS

TIMELESS LESSONS FOR PRAYER WARRIORS: CONFIRMING KAVANUAGH-
THE SPIRITUAL BATTLE

Copyright © 2019 Zeb Bradford Long

All rights reserved; however, any part of this book that may aid in discernment and prayer to advance the Gospel of Jesus Christ may be reproduced without seeking permission or acknowledging the author.

PRMI

EXOUSIA
PRESS

Published by PRMI Exousia Press, a ministry of the Presbyterian-Reformed Ministries International Dunamis Institute

Black Mountain, North Carolina, USA
www.dunamisinstitute.org

Cover design and graphics by Joe Schlosser, Excellent Adventures Inc.

Scripture quoted by permission. All scripture quotations, unless otherwise indicated, are taken from the NET Bible® copyright ©1996-2016 by Biblical Studies Press, L.L.C. All rights reserved.

Because of the dynamic nature of the Internet, any web addresses or links contained in this book may have changed since publication and may no longer be valid.

ISBN: 978-1-7339269-0-4

DEDICATION

To all the Dunamis Fellowship International intercessors who joined in this phase in the war for the Judeo-Christian soul of America in order that the United States as a nation and its citizens of biblical faith may continue to play a strategic role in the global advancement of the Kingdom of God.

"Who will stand up for me against evildoers? Who will take his stand for me against those who do wickedness?"
Psalm 95:16 ASV

The theme photograph is of an intercessory prayer team on a mountain overlooking the distant site of the 9/11/2001 Islamic terrorist attacks that destroyed the World Trade Towers and murdered 2,753 people.

ACKNOWLEDGMENTS

I acknowledge with thanksgiving my teacher in intercession, the Rev. Archer Torrey, the founder of the Anglican Prayer Community Jesus Abbey in South Korea, which for me was a laboratory and a "boot camp" for cooperating with the Holy Spirit in intercession and spiritual warfare.

Thanks to all those in the Presbyterian-Reformed Ministries (PRMI) and the Dunamis Fellowship International (DFI) prayer networks and cohorts who joined in this prayer battle and contributed to the writing of this book.

Special thanks to the editing team who worked on the manuscript: Judy Cook for meticulous editing of my dyslexic spelling and grammar, and encouraged me to keep writing. Helen Lowes who did editing of the overall flow of the book. Mary Ellen Conners on the PRMI leadership team for layout and preparation for publication.

I am indebted to the core leadership team of PRMI and the PRMI Board of Directors who provided the spiritual cover and support for me to not only do the work of prayer, but to reflect and write about it, so that the lessons learned may be passed on to future intercessors. Thanks to the Rev. Cindy Strickler the Director of PRMI and the DFI for her anointing to provide spiritual oversight of the ministry while I was deployed in these prayer battles.

Special thanks to my friend Steve Aceto an attorney, intercessor, discerner of spirits and a great analytical mind. Our conversations and participation in prayers battles together over the decades have profoundly shaped my thinking and ability to articulate the concepts in this book.

Lastly, I am so grateful to my wife the Rev. Laura Cole Long. What an extraordinary gift she is to me! It takes a special gift of God's love and grace to live with, me—a prayer warrior.

Chapter 1 The Context of the Confirmation Battle

Table of Contents

Chapter 1 The Context of the Confirmation Battle

1

The Context of the Confirmation Battle

The battle for the confirmation of Judge Brett Kavanaugh to the Supreme Court of the United States was a major revelatory event that exposed Satan's plans and tactics in the war for the soul of America. This struggle also revealed timeless tactics the Holy Spirit deploys in calling intercessors to defeat Satan's plans and advance the Kingdom of God.

Although there were human, political and ideological dimensions in this confirmation process, my focus is on revealing the spiritual dimension and the role of intercessory prayer.

From this perspective, the battle consisted of a series of prayer engagements that started on July 9, 2018 when President Trump announced Judge Brett Kavanaugh as his nominee to replace Justice Anthony Kennedy on the Supreme Court. The battle concluded on October 20th with a coven of witches in New York inviting the public to rituals in which to curse the newly appointed judge.

Throughout this entire battle, I was aware that the *Presbyterian-*

Reformed Ministry International (PRMI)[1] intercessors were only one very small part of a multifaceted concert of prayer. There were many groups who were engaged in this effort. This prayer work was coordinated by the Holy Spirit rather than any human central authority. PRMI intercessors took part in other prayer initiatives and shared the intelligence they received from those networks. The two most important for us were the POTUS Shield[2] and Intercessors for America.[3]

I became acutely aware throughout this struggle that we were only one unit in the army of intercessors involved in this campaign. From my limited perspective, I can only report what we were experiencing and how the Holy Spirit was working through our PRMI prayer team. This is not to inflate the importance of PRMI's role in the battle, nor to minimize the role of others. I just do not know how the Holy Spirit was directing these other units. Someday, at the Great Feast of the Lamb, we may see fully how all this prayer work fit together to advance God's Kingdom purposes.

Rights are Given by God, Not by Government

---

[1]*Presbyterian-Reformed Ministries International (PRMI)* was founded in 1966 as *Presbyterian Charismatic Communion*. (www.prmi.org) The ministry's purpose is to create the context where God the Father continues to fulfill Acts 1:4-8 so that Christians may be empowered by the Holy Spirit to be witnesses to Jesus Christ. Under PRMI is a global apostolic network called the *Dunamis Fellowship International* (DFI) with members from many nations, and branches in USA, Canada, United Kingdom, and South Korea. (https://www.prmi.org/ministries-of-prmi/dunamis-fellowship-intl/) The intercessors who took part in the Kavanaugh prayer battle reported in this book were participants in PRMI's equipping programs and active members of the DFI.

[2]https://www.potusshield.org/

[3]https://www.ifapray.org/

We must first view the battle for the confirmation of Judge Kavanaugh from the master strategy perspective. This places the battle within the context of the war for the soul of America.

To understand the political and spiritual battle fought around the Senate confirmation of Judge Kavanaugh to the Supreme Court, we must grasp the nature of America and our founding documents.[4] Ben Shapiro gives this brilliant summary of the historical sources of the values embodied in the Constitution:

> America was built on a fundamental idea—an idea that was the product of nearly three thousand years of philosophical evolution. That idea, planted at Sinai, watered in the Galilee, pruned through the thought of Athens and strengthened by the push and pull of reason and revelation for centuries, was embedded by our founders in the Declaration of Independence and the Constitution of the United States, and that principle was simple: that human beings are made in the image of God, that we are therefore beneficiaries of inalienable God-given rights, that government was created in order to protect those rights, not invade them, and that we must use our freedom to pursue virtue. God said to Pharaoh, "Let my people go so that they may worship me." The United States echoed that message from its very inception.[5]

---

[4] I have covered this extensively in another book exposing Satan's plans in which I describe the unique founding and structure of America and other nations based on our Judeo-Christian/Greek-born power of reason values which are so effective for constraining evil and providing for human freedom. I also lay out the overall battle plan of Satan which is essentially the replacement of those values with another set of values which come essentially from modern adaptations of Marxism. (As of January 2019, this is yet to be published.)

[5] https://www.dailywire.com/news/29901/watch-shapiro-champions-judeo-christian-values-daily-wire

The role of the Supreme Court in the US system of government is defined by the Constitution Section III as follows: "The judicial power shall extend to all cases, in law and equity, arising under this Constitution, the laws of the United States, and treaties made, or which shall be made, under their authority;..."[6]   In short, the Supreme Court is charged with implementing these laws within the framework of the Constitution and by doing so will uphold both the ideal of America and the Judeo-Christian/Greek-born power of reason values that defined that ideal.   However, it must be understood that the Supreme Court is not the ultimate guardian of the Constitution. Over the years, the US Supreme Court has more or less assumed the role of final determination as to whether laws and treaties are consistent with the Constitution of the United States. But the Constitution doesn't say that. Instead all branches of government and we the people are its guardians.[7] This is why we the people, through those whom we elect to office, have the responsibility to select judges for the Court who will interpret the Constitution in a way most consistent with the framers.

The vulnerable point in this entire system of governance has become how the justices who sit on the Supreme Court interpret the Constitution. One approach to interpretation is embodied in Judge Brett Kavanaugh as described in a statement from Leonard Leo, executive vice president of the Federalist Society, who wrote Trump's shortlist of nominees:

"Brett Kavanaugh is among the most distinguished and

---

[6]https://www.law.cornell.edu/constitution/articleiii

[7]This observation is from Steve Aceto who says it is a common misunderstanding that the Supreme Court is the guardian of the Constitution. Steve Aceto is an attorney, an intercessor and personal friend. He is a deep thinker and a gifted discerner of spirits. For decades the Lord has provided me with guidance and discernment through him.

respected judges in the country, with nearly 300 opinions that clearly demonstrate fairness and a commitment to interpreting the Constitution as it's written and enforcing the limits on government power contained in the Constitution."[8]

The article by Abigail Simon in Time magazine, "President Trump Picked Brett Kavanaugh for the Supreme Court. Who Is He?" from July 10, 2018, adds further definition to the perspective of interpreting the Constitution.

Kavanaugh has historically applied principles of textualism and originalism to cases—legal traditions that advocate for an interpretation of the Constitution based on the meaning that the text would have had at the time it was written.[9]

This implies that Judge Kavanaugh, by upholding the original meaning of the Constitution, upholds the Judeo-Christian/Greek-born power of reason values that are embodied within the Constitution.[10] Originalism includes, for example, the recognition that the first amendment does not guarantee freedom of religion, instead it prohibits laws that restrict the free expression of religion.

---

[8] https://www.axios.com/trump-nominates-brett-kavanaugh-supreme-court-justice-a0866ea4-0121-4451-b28d-620b00c67230.html

[9] http://time.com/5334098/donald-trump-brett-kavanaugh-supreme-court/ Also see https://www.merriam-webster.com/dictionary/textualism

[10] I am indebted to Ben Shapiro for this term, "The Greek Born-Power-of-Reason." His book, *The Right Side of History: How Reason and Moral Purpose Made the West Great*, Harper Collins Publishers (2019) brilliantly describes how the foundations of the West and America are found in the dynamic tension between (1) Jerusalem which embodies the role of God as creator, law giver and redeemer; and (2) Athens which embodies the power of human reason and purpose. From PragerU, an excellent five minutes video summary. https://youtu.be/RVD0xik-_FM.

The difference is enormous, and unique to the United States. Its effect should be to keep biblical faith—Judaism and Christianity—in the public square.

In contrast to this view held by Kavanaugh, are other judges who practice what is called "judicial activism." This is defined as follows:

> Judicial activism is a legal term that refers to court rulings that are partially or fully based on the judge's political or personal considerations, rather than on existing laws. In basic terms, judicial activism occurs when a judge presiding over a case allows his personal or political views to guide his decision when rendering judgment on a case.[11]

As a result, a judge who practices judicial activism may look outside of the Judeo-Christian/Greek-born power of reason values embodied in the Constitution for guidance in changing our nation's laws.

The trend of the last forty years has been for judges to take the approach of judicial activism, resulting in a set of decisions that have brought profound changes to American society. Take for instance cases of the removal of religious expressions of biblical faith from public places. Such actions are in opposition to the Framers intentions in the Frist Amendment which prohibits laws restricting the free expression of religion.

The rulings by activist judges are eroding this basic foundation of the Constitution intended to protect our God given rights in the First and Second Amendments with the effect of expelling biblical faith altogether, rather than simply being inclusive of others. The net result in removing our biblical faith foundations in Judaism and Christianity from the public space, the basis for our values upon which the nation is founded, prepares the way for those biblical values being replaced by anti-biblical values. The result will be the transformation of the United States of America into a nation very different from the one envisioned by the founders in the US

---

[11]https://legaldictionary.net/judicial-activism/

Declaration of Independence and the Constitution.

This was all dramatically illustrated when the Obama Administration sought to force the Little Sisters of the Poor (a Roman Catholic charity) to violate their religious convictions by providing birth control in their insurance plan. In another case, a Christian baker was charged by authorities for refusing to bake a cake for a gay marriage ceremony which was in opposition to his beliefs. Predating by decades the Obama administration, we have witnessed the removal from public spaces of Jewish and Christian symbols like the Ten Commandments, the Menorah, Nativity scenes, and the Cross. At the same time, it seems increasingly acceptable in the public square to have pagan symbols of Halloween or the symbols of non-biblical religions such as Islam.

The horrifying, verifiable reality is that our Judeo-Christian values embedded in the Constitution are being removed and replaced by another set of principles and ethics. These come not from God's revelation to humanity in the Bible, but from anti-God and anti-biblical, Satanic deception of dialectical materialism under many guises: Marxism, Socialism, Intersectionality and other ideologies from the same poisonous root that are presently in vogue, captivating the popular culture, the liberal media, and most ominously, the leadership of the Democratic Party. As the 20th century disasters of Communism and Nazism and the 21st century expressions of Marxism in Cuba, North Korea, and Venezuela clearly demonstrate, there are catastrophic consequences when those deceived by this ideology gain political power. If the same or similar ideologies continue to grow in America, then prospects are dire not only for this nation, but for the world.

Stopping and reversing these movements before they can bear their full bitter fruit for the nation and the Kingdom of God is the reason why God is calling intercessors into this battle to place originalist judges on the US Supreme Court. This is one decisive front in the war for the Soul of America.

The Roots of our Present Conflict in the American Revolution of 1776 and the French Revolution of 1789

The crux of the war for the soul of America and this present confirmation battle is the question of the source of our rights of "Life, Liberty and the pursuit of Happiness." Are these rights given us by God because we are created in His Image? Or are these rights created by human beings themselves through forming "social contracts" of family, tribe, and state.

This question is so foundational that we need to linger longer on this topic if we are to understand the nature of the war that we are in and the vicious opposition to President Trump nominating originalist judges to the courts. This will help us see why God called intercessors to engage in this battle both in the spiritual realm and in the messy sphere of partisan politics.[12]

In the battle to confirm Judge Kavanaugh, we are experiencing the convergence and clashing between two streams within human history and society. The first stream is embodied in the American Revolution of 1776, which growing out of Judeo-Christian values, contended that rights were given by God. This foundational conviction is expressed in the preamble of the Declaration of Independence.

> "We hold these truths to be self-evident, that all men are created equal, that they are endowed by their Creator with certain unalienable Rights, that among these are Life, Liberty and the pursuit of Happiness."[13]

---

[12] I am indebted to Steve Aceto for these insights.

[13] https://www.archives.gov/founding-docs/declaration

This is root from which the tree of Western culture and America has grown bearing the good fruit of freedom, equality, equal justice under the law, and prosperity.

The second stream is the secular French Revolution of 1789 which dethroned God, rejected Judeo-Christian values, and made the collective the giver of rights.[14] Ben Shapiro in his book *The Right Side of History* provides a summary of this replacement:

> The rejection of Judeo-Christian values and ancient virtue on behalf of the general will was expressed in glowing terms in the French Declaration of the Rights of Man, approved by the National Assembly on August 26, 1789. Unlike the Declaration of Independence—a document a expressing a collective desire for individual rights—the Declaration of the Rights of Man expresses the belief that man's place in the universe revolves around his role as a part of the larger collective. Every individual right expressed in the French Declaration is curbed by the collective's right to overrule that individual. So, for example, the French Declaration states, "Men are born and remain free and equal in rights. Social distinctions may be founded only upon the general good." But the second clause renders the first absolutely meaningless—if men are equal in right, how can their rights be subject to the opinions of a majority?
>
> The answer is obvious. In the French Declaration, rights do not spring from God or preexist government: "The principle of all sovereignty resides essentially in the nation. No body nor individual may exercise any authority which does not proceed directly from the nation." All rights come from the state. All

---

[14]For a far more complete analysis of the contrast between the French and American revolutions than I can offer, go to:
https://www.heritage.org/political-process/report/the-nature-rights-american-politics-comparison-three-revolutions.

rights therefore belong to the state. This is the Hobbesian Leviathan come to life.[15]

We must push forward to understand the spiritual dimensions of the American and French revolutions as they define the spiritual battle behind the confirmation of Judge Kavanaugh. The great Dutch theologian Abraham Kuyper brings to light the deep religious and biblical faith side of this issue of the source of our rights and the contrast between these two revolutions and spells out the consequences. Kuyper brings us to the roots of our "Judeo-Christian values" which is biblical faith as articulated in the Reformed Faith of Calvinism with its particular expression of Presbyterianism mingled with the Scottish Enlightenment, which exerted a pervasive influence upon the founders of America.

In his brilliant lectures on Calvinism given at Princeton Seminary in 1898, Kuyper contrasted the spiritual roots of the Dutch, English, and American Revolutions with those of the French Revolution. He exposes the different fruit.[16]

"The French Revolution is in principle distinct from all these national revolutions, [i.e., the three revolutions of the Reformed world: the Dutch, the English and the American] which were undertaken with praying lips and with trust in the help of God. The French Revolution ignores God. It opposes God. It refuses to recognize a deeper ground of political life than that which is found in nature, that is, in this instance, in man himself. Here the first article of the confession of the most absolute infidelity is—"ni Dieu ni

---

[15]Shapiro, Ben. *The Right Side of History: How Reason and Moral Purpose Made the West Great*, Broadside Books, HarperCollins Publishers, New York (2019) pp. 124-125.

[16]http://www.ccel.org/ccel/kuyper/lecture.html

maitre." [no God no master] The sovereign God is dethroned and man with his free will is placed on the vacant seat. It is the will of man which determines all things. All power, all authority proceeds from man."[17]

"In the sphere of Calvinism, as also in your *Declaration,* the knee is bowed to God, while over against man the head is proudly lifted up. But here, from the standpoint of the sovereignty of the people, the fist is defiantly clenched against God, while man grovels before his fellow men, tinseling over this self-abasement by the ludicrous fiction that, thousands of years ago, men, of whom no one has any remembrance, concluded a political contract, or, as they called it, *"Contrat Social...."*

"Now, do you ask for the result? Then, let History tell you how the rebellion of the Netherlands, the "Glorious Revolution" of England, and your own rebellion against the British Crown [The American Revolution] have brought liberty to honor; and answer for yourself the question: Has the French Revolution resulted in anything else but the shackling of liberty in the irons of State-omnipotence?"[18]

The historical validity of this profound observation by Kuyper, made in 1898 at the turn of the 19th century, is in the horrors, mass murder, and bondage visited on humanity when, with God dethroned, the state became omnipotent in fascism and communism in the 20th century.

You may ask: What does all this have to do with what is taking place in the battle rending the soul of America in the 21st century? Everything! This is the essential divide in our nation and in Western culture. In a culture, the "knee bowed to God" contains the seeds that may blossom into genuine equality and liberty for all human beings! But the "fist defiantly clenched against God" sows the wind

---

[17]Ibid, pp. 87-88.

[18]Ibid, p. 88.

that reaps the whirlwind of the absolute tyranny of a few men over all the others.

The spiritual aspect of the quest to put originalist justices on the Supreme Court is to uphold the foundational concept of rights given by God resulting in freedom and equality before the law for all.

In opposition to this goal are those whose "fists are defiantly clenched against God," resulting not in freedom and equality as they stridently proclaim, but in tyranny and inequality. The clenched fist is the universally recognized leftist symbol of confrontation!

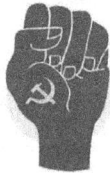

The self-identification symbol of Black Lives Matter, Communism and gay rights movements is the raised fist. This symbol was in evidence among the protesters against the Kavanaugh confirmation.

Those with fists clenched in defiance of God are a cultic force of diverse ideologies which are the successors of the French Revolution and which spring from its intellectual and spiritual roots. They go under many names—Marxism, dialectic materialism, Democratic Socialism, Radical Left, fascism, intersectionality, Radical Islam—all of which fit under the general category of "struggle ideologies."

These ideologies have the common thread of dethroning the God revealed in the Bible and the manufacture or deliberate escalation of conflict between races, religions, and other groups within society as a means of kingdom building. They are at their heart apocalyptic, but the kingdom coming after their version of apocalypse is not God's.[19]

Ominously, these struggle ideologies have increasingly captivated the popular culture and especially the leadership of the Democratic Party of the United States. Their influence is reflected in the 2012 Democratic Party platform where, echoing the French Revolution motto of "Liberté, égalité, fraternité," there was much talk of liberty, equality and justice, but all references to God were removed.[20] Once God is removed and humanity alone is sovereign, there are no constraints of God's law and judgement on our innate sinful tendencies. Despite humanities highest ideals, inexorably the door is opened to Satan who takes his seat behind the human collectives with no checks in place, leaving him free with his deceived human agents to seize absolute power by all means available to him. The result is atheistic, totalitarian regimes that create hells on earth.

The Divide Represented in the 2016 Election

As we entered the 2016 election season, movements seeking to replace the Judeo-Christian foundations of the American Republic, were gaining momentum and seemed unstoppable. During the

---

[19]Based on conversations from Steve Aceto who wrote me the following: How do we name ideology motivating those opposed to confirming Kavanaugh which illuminates their pernicious methods? "Marxist" is far too narrow to do justice to an ideology that goes back to fundamental enlightenment thinkers Kant and Hegel and passes through the French Revolution before it ever gets to Marx, not to mention that it is an overloaded and potentially distracting term. Consider the key word "struggle" as the result of a deliberate provocation of social conflict to achieve social and economic change. This use of the word would be instantly recognizable to Marxist true believers, whose task is to pit forces of "progress" against the forces of "reaction" resulting in "struggle" in which chaos eventually yields utopia - it's an apocalyptic religion substituted for our own biblical faith. In "struggle ideologies" or the "ideologies of struggle, truth and falsehood are exchanged for progress and reaction."

[20]https://www.theblaze.com/news/2012/09/04/dems-remove-all-references-to-god-from-2012-party-platform

primaries and presidential debates, I listened carefully to what each candidate said. I sought to discern whether they would play into Satan's hands by continuing the tendency of replacing Judeo-Christian values with values that excluded the 1776 foundation of God as the giver of our rights. Or would they uphold the Judeo-Christian values built into the founding documents of the United States? I also attempted to discern who would publicly state their intention of stopping and reversing judicial activism's replacement of these core founding convictions.

It was not until the Third Presidential Debate on October 20, 2016 (moderated by Chris Wallace of Fox News) that I could see clearly past all the campaign slogans and into the hearts and convictions of Hilary Clinton and Donald J. Trump. Chris Wallace posed the decisive question:

> "First of all, where do you want to see the court take the country? And secondly, what's your view on how the Constitution should be interpreted? Do the founders' words mean what they say or is it a living document to be applied flexibly according to changing circumstances."[21]

Hilary Clinton's response:

> "I have major disagreements with my opponent about these issues and others that will be before the Supreme Court. But I feel that at this point in our country's history, it is important that we not reverse marriage equality, that we not reverse Roe v. Wade, that we stand up against Citizens United, we stand up for the rights of people in the workplace, that we stand up and basically say: The Supreme Court should represent all of us. That's how I see the court, and the kind of people that I would be looking to nominate to the court would be in the great tradition of standing up

---

[21]https://www.politico.com/story/2016/10/full-transcript-third-2016-presidential-debate-230063

to the powerful, standing up on behalf of our rights as Americans. And I look forward to having that opportunity."

Donald Trump's response:

"I feel that the justices that I am going to appoint—and I've named 20 of them—the justices that I'm going to appoint will be pro-life. They will have a conservative bent. They will be protecting the Second Amendment. They are great scholars in all cases, and they're people of tremendous respect. They will interpret the Constitution the way the founders wanted it interpreted. And I believe that's very, very important. I don't think we should have justices appointed that decide what they want to hear. It's all about the Constitution of—of—and so important, the Constitution the way it was meant to be. And those are the people that I will appoint."

While Clinton was elegant in her prose, and Trump blunt and unpolished, the chasm gaped wide between them. Clinton not only acknowledged but committed to the activist approach and agenda in interpreting the Constitution. Trump, on the other hand, affirmed that he would appoint judges who would reverse those tendencies by staying true to the values and intentions of the founders embodied in the Constitution.

The statements made in the third debate revealed the true heart of the two candidates. This was the decisive dividing point. Clinton would be used by Satan to continue the course of removing and replacing God as the source of our rights and freedoms; Trump would be used by God to resist this replacement and to restore the US Constitution as the embodiment of our Judeo-Christian values.

For me, and I believe for millions of others, this was the reason we were led, despite all Trump's obvious character flaws, to vote for him instead of Clinton. Voting him in as President of the United States set the stage for a series of political and spiritual confrontations, which while acted out between those engaged in politics, were ultimately clashes between the Kingdom of God and the empire of Satan.

I believe that placing originalist judges on the Supreme Court of the United States is a strategic part of God's plans to preserve the Judeo-Christian values embodied in the Constitution of the United States. Indeed, it may be a primary goal God is intending to work through Donald J. Trump.

Satan, on the other hand, is intent on continuing his plans of replacing Judeo-Christian values embodied in the Constitution through preventing originalist judges from being appointed to the Supreme Court. So, when Trump made his second appointment of an originalist Judge to the Supreme court, which shifted the court in a conservative direction, both the political and spiritual battles commenced.

Context of the Global Movement of the Holy Spirit

This battle for the soul of America is important in itself as our Judeo-Christian/Greek-born power of reason values are worth preserving and fighting for. However, that does not fully account for why God would call intercessors into this particular battle and why this is not anything more than a clash between two American political parties. Or, under the guise of prayer, we intercessors are not just supporters of President Trump whose campaign slogan is "Make America Great Again." The role of the intercessors is not to be involved in American or any other nation's politics, but rather to be focused on praying in the advancement of the Kingdom of God and fulfilling the Great Commission. This is a mission that transcends politics and national boundaries.

I believe that this battle for Kavanaugh is just one skirmish in one stream of a global movement of the Holy Spirit advancing the Kingdom of God. This may be identified as the westward blowing wind of the Spirit that began with the outpouring of the Holy Spirit in Jerusalem 2000 years ago and is now returning to the city of Jerusalem in fulfillment of Old and New Testament prophecies, bringing us closer to the return of Jesus Christ.

This movement that the intercessors from PRMI/DFI have been called by God to take part in consists of four distinct tributaries or waves of the Holy Spirit:

1.) The Jews returning to the land of Israel and to faith in Yeshua the Messiah.

2. The Back to Jerusalem Movement among those of Confucian culture (Koreans, Japanese, and Chinese) taking the Gospel of Jesus Christ along the Silk Road through the heartlands of Islam.

3. A continuation of the Charismatic renewal (Roman Catholic, Orthodox, Protestant, and Pentecostal) bringing awakening in the Western world for fulfilling the Great Commission.

4. A wind of the Holy Spirit blowing in the "house of Islam" bringing Muslims to faith in Jesus Christ.[22]

I believe the work of prayer to confirm Judge Kavanaugh to the Supreme Court is part of this third great wave of the Holy Spirit in the Western world. Within this third wave, this battle is the result of a concert of prayer through which God is defeating Satan's plans to prevent the United States, Canada, and the United Kingdom from fulfilling their holy destinies of providing freedom and liberty to the nations, protecting Israel, and creating the context for those of biblical faith to have the freedom and resources to take part in the global advancement of the Kingdom of God. We are presently in a battle for the foundational Judeo-Christian/Greek-born power of reason values which form the foundations of these three great nations. This is the larger setting of the spiritual battle to confirm Kavanaugh.

Part of the complexity of this and the basis for the concern that we are just involved in a particular nation's politics is that the clash between the Kingdom of God and the empire of Satan is taking place in the spiritual realm, but also very much on earth within human society. This clash is always mediated through the political and social issues of the day.

---

[22] I describe these four great waves of the Holy Spirit as the conclusion of my book, *A Prayer Strategy for the Victory of Jesus Christ*: *Defeating the Demonic Strongholds of ISIS and Radical Islam*. PRMI Exousia Press, 2018.

It also needs to be noted that PRMI/DFI intercessors are called into other prayer battles within the other great streams of the movement of the Holy Spirit which are also taking place in heaven and on earth. For instance, we are called to pray for the defeat of the demonic stronghold growing in China that is oppressing the church and blocking Chinese participation in advancing the Kingdom of God. Intercessors are involved in each of these four great streams of Kingdom advancement in the world today. The timeless lessons of intercession learned in this one skirmish are applicable to the prayer work in all the others. This confirmation battle is but one part of God's master plan that the Gospel of Jesus Christ go to all nations.

The Four Prayer Engagements

The confirmation battle of Judge Kavanaugh for the intercessors had four distinct engagements, each one corresponding to human/political phases of the confirmation process.

These four engagements were as follows:

- The first engagement started on July 9th with President Trump's announcement that Judge Brett Kavanaugh was his pick for the Supreme Court. It also included the hearings conducted by the Senate Judiciary Committee whose proceedings were constantly interrupted by protesters in the galleries.

- The second engagement started on Sept. 16th when a cascade of allegations of sexual misconduct, alleged to have taken place in high school and college years, were made public against Judge Kavanaugh. Sept. 27th was the culmination of this prayer battle when both Dr. Ford (who accused the Judge of trying to rape her while in high school) and Judge Kavanaugh testified before the Senate Judiciary Committee.

- The third engagement started after September 28th when the Judiciary Committee voted to send Kavanaugh's confirmation to the Senate floor, with Sen. Jeff Flake calling for a one-week FBI investigation into the claims made against him. A week of waiting ensued while the FBI did its supplementary background check.

- The fourth prayer engagement was on October 6th when the Senate approved Judge Kavanaugh to the Supreme Court by a margin of 50 to 48. It was then that witch covens announced public rituals of speaking curses against Judge Kavanaugh, just as they had launched similar rituals for cursing President Trump.

The Holy Spirit called PRMI intercessors into the first three of these engagements. We were not called into the fourth engagement of breaking the witchcraft curses against the judge. Apparently, this anointing and responsibility shifted to a group of Catholic exorcists.

Each of the three engagements will be recounted from the perspective of the intercessors. Then each will be followed by an After-Action Review (AAR) in which we will describe what was learned. These lessons may be instructive for intercessors in future battles.

My purpose is to relate just enough information about the political maneuvering and debates taking place in order to frame the spiritual dynamics we were involved in. For a detailed analysis of the substance of the debates, the political maneuvering, and the role of the press, I recommend you review the news reports at the time. For balance, you will need to review both the liberal and conservative outlets, which I did do. But the most helpful sources for navigating through the fog of war to objective facts and deeper ideological dynamics, were reports from the Heritage Foundation, Ben Shapiro's The Daily Wire, Bill O'Reilly, and The Daily Caller. I know these are all from a conservative viewpoint, but I found the reporting from the more liberal press to be so driven by vicious hatred of Trump and the obvious commitment to prevent the appointment of anyone whom he might nominate, that their reporting was not objective, but amounted to being the propaganda agency of those opposed to the nomination.

The Alignment of Forces on the Eve of the Battle

On the eve of any battle, the armies of the two opposing sides take up their positions. These are usually shown on a map of the battlespace with markers locating the different units. Imagine, with the eyes of the Spirit, viewing the location of both natural and supernatural actors who were involved in the battle to either secure or to oppose the confirmation of Brett Kavanaugh to the US Supreme Court. This is a complex multidimensional battlespace that may be imagined as clashes taking place on the following levels:

The Clash on the Spiritual Level

This consists of the clash in the spiritual realm between God with the angelic host of heaven against the forces of evil opposition as described by St. Paul in Ephesians 6:12:

> For our struggle is not against flesh and blood, but against the rulers, against the powers, against the world rulers of this darkness, against the spiritual forces of evil in the heavens.

The Clash of Worldviews and Ideologies

The clash is between two opposing worldviews and ideologies. The first view is a Judeo-Christian worldview of rights coming from God expressed in the American Revolution and preserved in the US Constitution. The second view is that rights come from man as represented in the French Revolution and expressed in various dialectical ideologies. This approach has been embodied in various political and cultural movements of liberal progressivism, secular humanism, and the radical left and right.

The Political Realm

The two opposing worldviews were embodied in different political and cultural movements. These were seen in the Republicans on the Judiciary Committee who were supporting the nomination joined by those supporting the placement of originalist judges on the Court. In opposition were the Democrats on the Judiciary Committee who opposed the nomination joined by others who also opposed it. Their goal seemed generally to be to oppose anything and everything proposed by President Trump, and to continue placing activist Judges on the US Supreme Court.

Where were the Intercessors?

I know this is simplistic, but I hope it shows us clearly where our role was as intercessors. We were entirely at work within the spiritual realm. We were not engaged in the political battles, nor joining the promotion of any ideology or worldview perspective. We were not expressing our opinions in any meaningful way to influence the debate. For instance, we PRMI intercessors were not on the street protesting or in any way trying to influence public opinion, nor did we have any access in the halls of the Capital. We were not even there on site! Our work of prayer transcended all of these levels, and from the spiritual realm had an impact in the clashes that were taking place at each level.

With this introduction let us move into the first engagement.

Chapter 1 The Context of the Confirmation Battle

2

First Engagement: Piercing the Cloaking

The call to pray for Judge Brett Kavanaugh came on July 9, 2018 when President Trump publicly introduced the Judge, along with his wife and their two daughters.[23]

JuleAnn, an intercessor, reported the way the Holy Spirit forewarned her of the terrible ordeal that the Kavanaugh family was about to endure: "When I saw that lovely family standing there, the Holy Spirit fell upon me and called me into the gap to pray for them. The Lord said, "Pray for grace and for protection for them for the fiery ordeal that is ahead."

However, for many intercessors, the first major engagement did not begin until September 4, 2018 with the start of the Senate Judiciary Committee hearings. These began at 9:30 AM in the Hart Senate Office Building. The hearings were chaired by Senator Chuck Grassley (R-Iowa).

---

[23]https://www.axios.com/trump-nominates-brett-kavanaugh-supreme-court-justice-a0866ea4-0121-4451-b28d-620b00c67230.html

I did not attend the hearings, but watched the live stream broadcast that took place in Room 216 of the chambers of the Capital Complex. I also constantly checked news reports of what was taking place. It quickly became apparent this was not going to be business as usual.

Crowds of protestors gathered in Washington. Inside the committee hearings, it became obvious that the Democrats were unified in their opposition to Judge Kavanaugh and were attempting many delay tactics, such as demanding more information and documentation. Many questions were asked. There was considerable debate between the Republican and Democratic committee members as well.

Judge Kavanaugh seemed to be holding up extremely well under the often hostile grilling. Debate and cross examination are a normal and healthy part of our democratic process. However, what was not normal or conducive to the rational democratic process were the frenzied protests occurring inside and outside of the building. Protesters in the gallery audience relentlessly interrupted the deliberations. They were especially irrational and disorderly when the Judge attempted to answer the senators' questions, or when the Republican members of the committee were trying to speak.

I observed this activity for myself through live streaming. I also read reports in the news confirming this disruptive behavior. But most helpful to me was a personal source of information, a young man named Jon Brown, who was in Washington, DC working as an intern for a news organization. He is anointed by the Holy Spirit, and has gifts of observation and spiritual discernment coupled with a talent for journalism. During these engagements, Jon gave me first hand updates of what he observed, as well as describing the spiritual atmosphere. He wrote the following about the protesters and their tone: "Every few minutes the hearings are interrupted by some shrill insane protestor, who is subsequently dragged out of the hearing room and arrested. This goes on all day. It is truly disgraceful."

Some seemed to discount the reports of the protesters as being overly exaggerated. One Democratic senator dismissed the disruptions as just "democracy in action."[24] However, it seemed that what was going on was intended to destroy our democratic process. To me, the protests seemed too organized and orchestrated to just be citizens exercising the freedom to express their political opinions.

I was also disturbed to find Linda Sasour, an American political activist and advocate for imposing Islamic Shariah Law, playing a leading role in the protest. On the September 8th live stream, she was observed shrieking and screaming unintelligible words, then struggling while being dragged out by the police, only to return and do a repeat performance. The very fact that she was there leading the opposition of an originalist judge exposes the deep agenda of both the Islamists and the Radical Left of using activist judges to advance their values which are contrary to those of the founders of our country embodied in the Constitution.

Most of the protesters appeared to be focused on upholding Roe vs Wade and abortion rights. But it appeared to me that this was used as the hot issue to mobilize the demonstrators. To me, it seemed like the abortion issue and woman's rights issues were a Trojan Horse carrying the deadly virus of Radical Left Marxist and Islamic ideology.

Receiving Guidance as to How to Pray

After concluding that these protests were actually taking place and were as disruptive as they appeared to be, I sent out the following prayer to the Discerning the Times Intercessors:

"Lord, in the power of Your Name, reveal what is taking place. Come, Holy Spirit, and pierce the cloaking hiding the human schemes, and behind them the schemes of Satan."

No sooner had we prayed this piercing-the-cloaking prayer, then dubious aspects of the protests were exposed.

---

[24]@CoryBooker

The first revelation was that many of the protesters were being paid to be disruptive. I gathered this from news reports I was reading. One was from several doctors from Texas who were on site: An article from the Western Journal provides evidence of this activity. In a video, one of the doctors reported:

"Hello, I'm Dr. Tom Schlueter from Texas. We came here to participate in the hearings, to get in the line," one said.

"One of the things was, there were people who had come along... who had a bag of money, and people would hand them a piece of paper, and then they would give them money. So, we know money was exchanged for some of the people to be here, just to protest.

"There was no depth to what their understanding was or anything. They were just here to be a protester. They were actually told, we heard them say this and instruct them, 'When you go in, we want you to yell, to scream, and even possibly get arrested.' So that was some of the processes we saw happening..." Another backed him up.[25]

I read this article, watched the video clip, and concluded that these doctors from Texas were Christians who had been called to be on site to pray for the hearings.[26]

That this was orchestrated, and that people were being paid to protest was further confirmed by Jon Brown, my young reporter friend who was on site. He had asked for prayer that he could get some confirmation of the rumor that protesters were in fact being paid. He wrote:

"Today on Twitter I found pictures of a person shoveling cash out of an envelope to a woman who had been kicked out. I was able to find out who he is. He is employed by a far-left activist group funded by George Soros. Soros is behind much

---

[25]https://www.westernjournal.com/ct/protesters-paid-say-3-doctors/
[26]https://youtu.be/3-ZlfUbRSal

of the turmoil in this country. He is trying to destroy our democratic institutions."

The journalist asked for prayer that he could get full verification of this activity and that it could be exposed to the American public. While the Washington Post and other liberal media denied that the protesters were being paid, we started to get confirmation from unlikely sources in the liberal media.[27] A USA Today article published on September 5, 2018 named organizations behind the protest. Among them was the Center for Popular Democracy and others who received support from George Soros.[28] The information we were receiving strongly suggested that there was a larger organization and movement supporting and enabling these protests.[29] This was anything but grassroots outrage.

Satan's Plans Stirring up the Marxist/Hegelian Dialectic

We were all praying according to this guidance and moving intensely into the battle. The intercessors continued to receive guidance: For instance, JuleAnn wrote:

"I believe I heard clearly from the LORD, 'There is a strategic, orchestrated plan set in an attempt to disrupt this nomination.' It was obvious the form of tactics that are being used are of anarchy. It feels similar to the dynamic of stirring

---

[27]https://www.washingtonpost.com/politics/2018/10/05/no-george-soros-isnt-paying-kavanaugh-protesters/?utm_term=.aa25ff114c4e

[28]https://www.usatoday.com/story/news/politics/2018/09/05/brett-kavanaugh-hearing-disruptions-testimony-coordinated-supreme-court/1201785002/

[29]Grassroots outrage? Soros-funded activists behind anti-Kavanaugh campaign. Published time: 4 Oct, 2018 12:47. Edited time: 5 Oct, 2018 08:07 https://www.rt.com/usa/440314-kavanaugh-soros-popular-democracy/

up by two sides both filled with hatred in Charlottesville at the protest over the Confederate war memorials."

Kim in New York affirmed JuleAnn's comment about what was taking place:

"I believe what we are watching is a slow train wreck into lawlessness. Opponents enrage each other over perceived lapses in social standards. Talking heads and ephemeral leaders intimidate and foment violence. Mob rule and even assassination are being hinted at by some."

This dialogue of discernment and engagement in prayer constantly continued between us over the internet and through telephone calls. As I was praying into all this, waves of fear swept over me as I saw the hatred and anarchy disrupting our democratic process. JuleAnn's word that it felt similar to Charlottesville alerted us to realize that we were again seeing the Marxist/Hegelian dialectic being stirred up. The intention was to block the rational debate and due process necessary for the confirmation of Judge Kavanaugh.

A Further Call to Intercession

Based on what we were seeing and discerning, the Holy Spirit led us to pray in the following ways:

- We were called to pray for those people praying on site at the hearings to be able to discern spirits, tell the truth, and intercede—like the three doctors from Texas, my journalist friend, representatives from Intercessors of America, and no doubt many others.

- We were called to bind and expel the demons who had been invited into the location and into various chambers of

Congress.
- We were also praying for God the Father to use what Satan and his human agents had intended for evil, to instead work to advance His Kingdom plans.

As we prayed into all of this, I do not think any of us were experiencing much demonic pushback. It was just intense and relentless. We believed we were seeing the results of our prayer work mostly in the way that the confirmation hearings were not derailed, but continued on. Despite the disruptions and the relentless, sometimes hostile questioning from the Democrats, Judge Kavanaugh seemed to be doing very well in answering the questions. His responses were measured and wise, and reflected his judicial philosophy. He did not fall into the traps set for him because he refused to give opinions on hypothetical cases.[30] He also gave some excellent teaching on constitutional law and how our judicial system is intended to function. It seemed that the deliberations were moving toward a vote by the Judiciary Committee, which would no doubt be along party lines to recommend Judge Kavanaugh go before the entire Senate to be confirmed. This felt like the answer to prayers. We were moving from intercession into praise and thanksgiving.

Then on September 16, in what felt very much like a surprise attack, the Washington Post published an article in which a Dr. Christian Ford made allegations against Judge Kavanaugh. She alleged that while at a party in high school, a drunken Kavanaugh and his friend Mark Judge pushed her into a bedroom where Kavanaugh pinned her down, attempted to remove her clothing, and held his hand over her mouth. She believed that as she tried to scream for help, he attempted to rape her.[31] This first exposé

---

[30]https://www.foxnews.com/politics/kavanaugh-cites-ginsburg-rule-in-declining-certain-questions-during-confirmation-hearing-what-is-it

was followed by allegations of even more egregious sexual I sconduct by Brett Kavanaugh while in high school and college. These allegations launched us into the next prayer engagement.

Before moving into the second engagement, we must step back and do an After-Action Review of this first engagement.

---

[31]How we got here: The Kavanaugh timeline - https://www.axios.com/brett-kavanaugh-timeline-allegations-vote-412d33d6-e5dd-43eb-9322-fd2a3867be9b.html

3

First Engagement: After-Action Review

In order to pass on what we have learned from the engagements to intercessors who are called into future battles, we conclude each phase of the battle with an After-Action Review.

You, of course, may choose to skip these chapters and continue to read the narrative of the prayer engagements. These are certainly a lot more exciting and interesting to read (and for me, to write) than what can at times be the tedious work of analyzing the spiritual dynamics that took place. However, I hope you will stay with me in these chapters.

My intention is to extract from these battles the timeless lessons of how to cooperate with the Holy Spirit in deploying the tactics of intercession and spiritual warfare to defeat Satan's schemes and to advance the Kingdom of God. This will help prepare you for the battles you may be called to engage in.

What is an After-Action Review?

It has been the practice of PRMI for many years, that whenever the Holy Spirit has moved during an event or demons have manifested, we pause and do a "debriefing." This is an occasion to reflect together on what the Holy Spirit was doing and allow people to ask questions about what they have observed. As we go through this process together, we often find the dynamics of the working of the Holy Spirit becoming clear. By regularly doing this analysis, we cultivate the gifts of discernment and learn how to cooperate with the Holy Spirit as a team.

I described this process to my son-in-law right after he returned from deployment as a platoon leader in Iraq. He said, "Yes, that is just what we do after an engagement with the enemy, except we call it an, 'After-Action Review' or an AAR." He explained, "We all discuss together what the enemy was up to, how we responded, and how we could have done better. This approach turns our combat experiences into great learning experiences that make us more effective soldiers and better at defeating the enemy's tactics."[32]

He referred me to the US Army Combat manual where I found the following:

Modern combat is complex and demanding. To fight and win, we must train our soldiers during peacetime to successfully execute their wartime missions. We must use every training opportunity to improve soldier, leader, and unit task performance. To improve their individual and collective-task performances to meet or exceed the Army standard, soldiers and leaders must know and understand what happened or did not happen during every training event. After-action reviews

---

[32]In a personal conversation with Major Adam Schultze, Artillery Office in the US Army.

(AARs) help provide soldiers and units feedback on mission and task performances in training and in combat. After-action reviews identify how to correct deficiencies, sustain strengths, and focus on performance of specific mission essential tasks list (METL) training objectives.[33]

This is a great description of what intercessors and spiritual warriors need to do after a prayer engagement. Therefore, I have replaced the term *debriefing* with *after-action review* as a better description of the process. By reflecting together as a team, we are able to deepen our discernment of the Devil's tactics. We also learn how to better cooperate with the Holy Spirit and one another in defeating Satan and in staying on track with God's plans. Out of this process of review and analysis, we are able to distill from our prayer battles timeless lessons to pass on to other intercessors.

Ideally, After-Action Reviews take place with the prayer team face to face. But PRMI intercessors involved in the prayer battle to confirm Judge Kavanaugh were scattered across the USA, UK, and Canada. So we had to do our debriefings over conference calls, emails, and text messages. My role in this prayer battle was to ask the intercessors to join in this process of reflecting on what had happened. I then was joined by Martin Boardman, PRMI Prayer Mobilizer, and other PRMI intercessors in distilling the lessons learned. Often, I was so consumed with the battle and/or recovering from the battle that I had to depend upon Martin to maintain the communication system and sort through the barrage of information coming in.

What we learn from these prayer battles is timeless. While circumstances constantly change, the nature of Satan and his tactics, as well as man's fallen human nature, remain constant

---

[33]For the complete manual go to http://www.au.af.mil/au/awc/awcgate /army/tc_25-20/tc25-20.pdf.

throughout all ages. The schemes of Satan and tactics of the Holy Spirit that are clarified through After-Action Reviews are like the basic notes of music, able to be endlessly adapted in different circumstances. Once you understand and have mastered the basic dynamics of cooperating with the Holy Spirit, the tactics of intercession and spiritual warfare, you can effectively deploy them in different situations. My intention in passing this on to future intercessors and spiritual warriors is to prepare them for the battles with Satan that we will be engaged in until our Lord Jesus Christ returns in glory and brings a definitive end to this war.

Defining a Prayer Engagement

We already identified in Chapter 1 that the battle to confirm Judge Brett Kavanaugh to the Supreme Court involved four engagements. It is important to grasp an understanding of prayer engagements.

I get the term *engagement* from the Prussian general and historian Carl von Clausewitz (1780–1831) the author of *On War.* He defines a military campaign as consisting of a series of specific encounters with the enemy which he calls *engagements.* Each campaign takes place over a specific length of time to accomplish certain objectives. For instance, in a military campaign, the objective for fighting may be to take and hold a hilltop fortification or thwart the enemy from breaking through one's lines of defense. In a spiritual battle, the objective of an engagement is understood as intercessors *stepping into the gap* to do the work of prayer intercession and accomplish the specific objectives of the Lord's battle plan. In the Kavanaugh hearings, a specific engagement was to pray in the name of Jesus to expose and bind the demonic powers that were energizing the protesters.

Two biblical examples of intercessors are Moses and Jesus who continually lived out the call and role of intercessor in their lives. But the actual work of intercession took place in those moments when they obediently stepped into the gap in prayer.

The term *stepping into the gap* comes from Psalm 106 which

described the events of Exodus 32:1-35. When Moses came down from Mount Horeb with the Ten Commandments, he discovered that the people had built a calf of gold and were worshipping it. God's wrath was about to break out against the people. But Moses pleaded with God not to destroy the people by reminding Him of the covenant He had made with Abraham, Isaac, and Israel. The result is stated in Exodus 32:14 TLV, "So Adonai relented from the destruction that He said He would do to His people." This work of Moses standing before God is the work of intercession as described in Psalm 106:23. A number of versions reflect the original Hebrew writing as, Moses "stood in the breach before Him."[34] Another translation of the word *breach* is *gap*.[35] The phrase *stepping into the gap*, therefore, has become a way to describe an intercessor's call to stand between the people and God in order to plead their case. It also includes standing between God's people and the Devil.

Another example of Moses standing in the gap is found in Exodus 17 at the battle of Amalek. As he stood on the hill top with his arms raised to the throne of the Lord with the assistance of Aaron and Hur, Joshua led his army to victory over the Amalekites in the valley below. Jesus Christ, as our intercessor, also steps into the gap. This is beautifully illustrated when He prayed to the Father at the tomb of Lazarus in John Chapter 11. Jesus stands *in the gap* between Lazarus and the powers of death and announces to all humanity that He is the resurrection and the life.   But above all, the greatest intercessory act of Jesus, His decisive engagement, was when He stood in the gap between a fallen humanity and the wrath of God, took our sin upon Himself and died on the cross. If we place our trust in Him, His offer of the gift of forgiveness and eternal life are ours.

---

[34]Psalms 106:23 TLV So He commanded their extermination, had not Moses, His chosen one, stood in the breach before Him, to turn His wrath from destroying them.

[35]H6556 perets peh'-rets From H6555; a break (literally or figuratively): - breach, breaking forth (in), X forth, gap. Strong's Hebrew and Greek Dictionaries.

Chapter 3 After Action Review: The First Engagement

From our spiritual perspective, an engagement takes place when an intercessor steps into the gap and joins the conflict in both the heavenly and earthly realms. This clash is between Satan, demons, and deceived human beings on one side; and the Holy Spirit, the angels, and redeemed human beings on the other.

From our human perspective, these conflicts are usually experienced as taking place within a specific period of chronological time in which certain objectives are met. Victory is either won for the Kingdom of God or gained for Satan. The engagements discussed in this book shall describe some of the objectives that were obtained, such as Kavanaugh being affirmed by the Senate Judiciary Committee and exposing that there was no truth in the allegations brought against the Judge. Each of these engagements and their specific results took place within discreet periods of time. However, this aspect of time gets complicated because these engagements also intersect with the spiritual realm.

Each engagement is linked in a series that contributes toward the goals of the overall battle. Clausewitz summarizes the results of this principle as follows:

> "By looking on each engagement as part of a series, at least insofar as events are predictable, the commander is always on the high road to his goal. The forces gather momentum, and intentions and actions develop with a vigor that is commensurate with the occasion, and impervious to outside influences."[36]

At the close of this book you will see how each spiritual engagement and its obtained objectives led to and made possible the next phase of the struggle. For instance, the engagement that resulted in Kavanaugh being approved by the Senate Judiciary Committee led to the next engagement that took place before the vote of the entire Senate. We may look back with 20/20 hindsight

---

[36]von Clausewitz, Carl, *On War,* Princeton University Press, New Jersey (1976) p. 182.

think the outcome of each engagement leading to Senate confirmation was foreordained by God, and therefore was inevitable. That, however, is not the way God works His will and intentions on earth. This is a real battle; the outcome depending upon our faith and obedience to God. Our courage and bold actions in both the spiritual and earthy battlespaces determine defeat or victory.

Each engagement is usually followed by a time of rest and preparation for the next engagement. For the spiritual warrior, this often requires spending time with God, but also with brothers and sisters who are alive in Christ for worship, prayer, confession and healing. The intercessor must also return to the normal world of family, work, church, and community. Without this return to normal life, the intercessor may become unbalanced and lose the ability to discern reality.

The concept of engagement is most helpful for understanding the dynamics of how the Holy Spirit calls us into periods of great intensity and conflict. Then, when His goals are achieved, we are allowed to step out of the intensity. This process or rhythm of engagement and disengagement accords with the physical limitations of our humanity. It is impossible, even with the anointing of the Holy Spirit, to indefinitely sustain the intensity required for these encounters within the spiritual realm.

The Tactics of Praying for the Holy Spirit to Pierce the Cloaking that Hides Satan's Plans and Purposes

In each of the four engagements involved in the battle to confirm Judge Brett Kavanaugh to the Supreme Court, we were led by the Holy Spirit to apply the tactic we called, "piercing Satan's cloaking." This tactic is based on how Satan works to form demonic strongholds. A stronghold is a human-demonic social organization that provides Satan, who is spirit, with the human, political, financial, and sometimes military means to carry out his purposes on earth. For instance, for Satan to carry out his terrible plan to exterminate the Jewish people, he built the demonic stronghold of

Nazism. For a complete and systematic description of demonic strongholds, how they are formed, and the way Satan works through them on earth, I recommend you read my book *A Prayer Strategy for the Victory of Jesus Christ*.

When a demonic stronghold is first formed, it is vulnerable to having its true purposes, plans, and humans involved exposed. And if exposed, then they can be countered. For example, if the German people and the nations of France, Great Britain, and America had known the full horrors of what Satan had planned through Hitler and the Nazi party, they would have risen in unison and destroyed this monster while it was still a helpless infant. In fact, there were prescient souls such as Rees Howells and Winston Churchill who foresaw the evil that was growing in Nazi Germany. But their dire warnings were ignored by people blinded to the ominous militarism and virulent hatred of the Jews growing in Germany. This blindness was the intentional work of Satan cloaking his activities and plans in Hitler and the Nazi party

This cloaking work takes place in all of Satan's activities, starting with the deception in our own hearts. But it can extend to the corporate sphere of organizations as well as political and social movements. The purpose of the cloaking is first of all to hide Satan's evil intentions from his victims and agents. Furthermore, it hides his intentions and work from all those who might interfere, those with cultural, political, and/or spiritual authority, including intercessors whom God has entrusted with the responsibly to work for the good of human society and the advancement of the Kingdom of God.

This cloaking is complex and works both within and outside of a stronghold. Within a stronghold, it functions like a "strong delusion" in which Satan darkens people's minds to prevent them from seeing. The cloaking is also maintained within the culture of a stronghold by attitudes and prohibitions that prevent any critical thought or criticism of Satan's woven structure of deception. The delusion and prohibitions are reinforced by harsh, institutionalized methods of silencing anyone who violates these taboos.

Outside of a stronghold, the cloaking works to prevent the true purposes, goals, means, and actions of a stronghold from being seen and understood by those who are either it's intended victims, or those who may have the power to expose, destroy, or prevent the stronghold from accomplishing Satan's purposes. Satan utilizes a diverse arsenal to provide the cloaking. Secrecy and distortion of facts by those within the stronghold keep it hidden. A worldview held by those outside the stronghold which cannot imagine the evil Satan intends, or which dismisses the role of religious faith keeps people blinded. In our present situation, Satan uses the irrational hatred of President Trump, the rejection of anything he proposes among the Radical Left and some in the Democratic party, as well as the uncritical approval of Trump among some of his more zealous followers, to prevent rational analysis and discernment of the demonic stronghold being formed in our nation. I believe the extreme polarization largely cultivated by the Radical Left is all part of Satan's cloaking to blind us as a nation to his plans for our destruction being carried out under our noses.

Demonic cloaking is essential to the formation of Satan's strongholds, especially in the beginning stages of their construction before obtaining the earthly power for self-defense or imposing their view of reality upon others.

Due to the pervasiveness of demonic cloaking, the first strategy intercessors must apply before entering into any engagement is prayer. Piercing the cloaking will expose Satan's plans and intentions, reveal who Satan's demonic and human agents are, and disclose how he is working through them. There are a number of specific tactics for piercing this demonic cloaking.

In this first engagement of the battle to confirm Kavanaugh to the Supreme Court, some of the tactics we were led to apply were as follows:

- A first tactic was to ask the Lord to expose the true plans of Satan being implemented through the protesters, and expose the human agents involved.

- A second tactic was to pray for some people to receive

prophetic vision to see into what was actually taking place in the spiritual realms.

- A third tactic was to command the evil spirits present in the hearings, on the streets, and working through the people and organizations, to expose their presence and their intentions.

After being led by the Holy Spirit to pray these piercing the cloaking prayers, one may experience God's answers through observations of the events that follow, some of which may reveal what is taking place below the surface. One must listen carefully to those who, either through prophetic vision or astute analysis of the facts, are exposing both the human and demonic plans and tactics.

Some of this is revealed during the prayer engagement which provides invaluable, actionable intelligence to guide our prayer. At other times, the full understanding of what is revealed must await the After-Action Review when the intercessors have the space to step back and reflect upon what has taken place and assess the information that has been exposed.

In the Kavanaugh hearings, we saw this dynamic exposed by the verified fact that the protesters were being paid to disrupt the Senate hearings. There were other revelations that were also received, but we waited for further verification of confirmed facts during the After-Action Review. The first of these was the revelation that the purpose of the protests was not just to prevent the confirmation of an originalist judge, but to ignite the Marxist/Hegelian dialectic to bring the destruction necessary to bring about their envisioned utopia. A second revelation was the confirmation that demons were actually manifesting in the protests and the disruptions that were taking place.

The Human and Spiritual Dangers of the
Marxist/Hegelian Dialectic

Some may scoff at the idea that a few paid protesters who were disrupting a hearing could be a matter of national and Kingdom concern. But to me, it is both deeply disturbing and alarming. I believe it is evidence of a strategy of Satan named the Marxist/Hegelian dialectic. This is the strategy of sowing conflict that can lead to anarchy. Its intention is the disruption of the orderly functioning of the democratic process.

We saw this same dynamic working through the protest and counter-protest in Charlottesville in 2017. The dynamic also surfaced in Portland in June and July 2018 with clashes between Antifa, an extreme left-wing group, and a group called Patriot Prayer who were described as right-wing.[37] Its dangerous currents were also at work in the Kavanaugh confirmation process. Such an orchestrated conflict is meant to cause the democratic government to fail and cease to function. The resulting anarchy would create ideal conditions for imposing some form of tyranny.

In the exposure of the intentional stirring up of chaos, we are seeing the master plan of both Satan and his human agents in action. As the rise of Nazism and Communism in the 20th century both demonstrated, this strategy is devastatingly effective. Intercessors, as well as those in government, must be aware of this strategy now being applied in 21st century America by the demonic strongholds of the Radical Left and Radical Right, and by Radical Islam.

---

[37]See "Organized Anarchy may soon Erupt in Portland," a Discerning the Times article. https://discernwith.us/organized-anarchy-may-soon-erupt-in-portland

Exposing the Presence of Evil Spirits

As we watched the protests, felt the tone of the hearings, and observed the way the liberal press amplified any opposition to Kavanaugh, we sensed an irrational and demonic dimension. It felt to me and other intercessors like the protestors were actually invoking and welcoming demonic spirits to manifest their presence and cause anarchy and confusion. Out of further reflection, I drew the following conclusion:

The orchestrated chaos (of the Marxist/Hegelian Dialectic) is the invoking of demonic spirits who aggravate the human situation and empower it for Satan's purposes. The significance of the location of the protests being in the United States Senate building and around the Capital (the symbols and context of representative democratic government) is conducive to these purposes. Besides the political and social implications, the intentional creation of anarchy within the chambers of the Capital Complex serve as evocations of high-level demonic spirits of Lawlessness and the Antichrist. (2 Thessalonians 2:7, and 1 John 4:3) Once high-level demons are welcomed in, they intensify the power of evil and usher in other demons. The lower-level demons then work through deceived human beings to build a demonic stronghold that will advance Satan's purposes on earth. This, however, raises the question of how we can know there really were high-level evil spirits energizing the protesters and the opposition to Kavanaugh's confirmation.

Confirming the Demonic Dimensions of the Protests

A fundamental principle of discernment is that as the Kingdom of God advances, it pushes back the empire of Satan. When this occurs, a power encounter takes place and demons are forced to manifest their presence and be driven out. This principle is given us by Jesus.

So, if Satan casts out Satan, he is divided against himself. How then will his kingdom stand? (27) And if I cast out demons by Beelzebul, by whom do your sons cast them out? For this reason they will be your judges. (28) But if I cast out demons by the Spirit of God, then the kingdom of God has already overtaken you. (Matthew 12:26-28)

The Kavanaugh confirmation hearing was the setting of a power encounter between Satan's empire and the Kingdom of God. This was first set up by President Trump nominating a devout Roman Catholic and godly man, an originalist judge committed to upholding the original meaning of the Constitution, as his choice for the Supreme Court. This stands in opposition to Satan's schemes. Not only were the protesters and Radical Left organizations supporting them opposed to Trump's choice, but the demonic powers behind them were also enraged. A national prayer movement which focused on praying that Trump would be empowered to fulfill his campaign pledge to nominate judges who would uphold the Constitution invited in the movement of the Holy Spirit. When Trump kept his promise through the nomination of Kavanaugh, the Holy Spirit orchestrated a national concert of prayer focused on the Judge, his family, and the confirmation process. This massive outpouring of prayer invited both the movement of the Holy Spirit and angelic protection into the proceedings. This triggered a clash with demonic and human powers invested in imposing their agenda to destroy and replace America's foundational Judeo-Christian values which were standing in their way.

Prayers for piercing the cloaking were being answered through the convergence of prayer movements who invited in the presence of Jesus Christ and countered the plans of Satan. This caused demons who were hidden behind human movements and politics to be driven into manifesting their presence. The result was evidenced in the frenzied, irrational tone of the protesters and the antagonistic, unreasonable opposition coming from Democratic senators.

In the engagements that followed, demonic entities manifested their presence and tactics as frenzied attempts to block the confirmation by bringing more and more outrageous and uncorroborated charges against the Judge. I experienced the manifestation of the demonic as a whirlwind in the media and the hearings. It was also reflected in the way the protesters roused the entire process into chaos and confusion. Many witnessed normally rational senators oppose the nomination by casting aside all due process and the assumption of innocence until proven guilty, creating a kangaroo court to unjustly destroy an innocent man and to subvert the rational confirmation process of advice and consent of a judge to the Supreme Court.

Confirmations of the irrational, demonic, and evil dimensions that took place were found in the actual facts of how the hearings progressed. These will be fully exposed in the next chapters. However, one surprising confirmation came from Peggy Noonan in "Opinion | *Voices of Reason—and Unreason:* Susan Collins put on a clinic in thoroughness and justice. Democrats need to stand up to the screamers." This article was published in the Wall Street Journal on October 11, 2018.

A word on the destructive theatrics we now see gripping parts of the Democratic Party. The howling and screeching that interrupted the hearings and the voting, the people who clawed on the door of the court, the ones who chased senators through the halls and screamed at them in elevators, who surrounded and harassed one at dinner with his wife, who disrupted and brought an air of chaos, who attempted to thwart democratic processes so that the people could not listen and make their judgments:

Do you know how that sounded to normal people, Republican and Democratic and unaffiliated? It sounded demonic. It didn't sound like "the resistance" or #MeToo. It sounded like the shrieking in the background of an old audiotape of an exorcism.[38]

Peggy Noonan is Roman Catholic, and I suspect, a born-again believer in whom the Holy Spirit dwells.[39]   She is providing a confirming witness to what many Spirit-filled PRMI intercessors discerned: Evil spirits were indeed present and being driven to manifest similarly to what happens during a deliverance or exorcism.

Let us now move back into the prayer battle by going to the next engagement in which the conflict heightens.

---

[38]*Voices of Reason—and Unreason: Susan Collins put on a clinic in thoroughness and justice. Democrats need to stand up to the screamers.*
https://www.wsj.com/articles/voices-of-reasonand-unreason-1539299053?mod=searchresults&page=1&pos=1

[39]She is a practicing Roman Catholic and attends St. Thomas More Church on Manhattan's Upper East Side.
https://en.wikipedia.org/wiki/Peggy_Noonan

Chapter 3 After Action Review: The First Engagement

Second Engagement: Phase 1—Gathering the Prayer Cohort

As intercessors, we felt the hearings were coming to a positive conclusion. It seemed to be smooth sailing for the Judiciary Committee to recommend Brett Kavanaugh for confirmation to the Senate.

Then, on September 16, the ambush took place. The Washington Post published an article in which a Dr. Christine Ford alleged that while she was in high school, a drunken Kavanaugh and his friend Mark Judge pushed her into a bedroom at a party. She further alleged that Kavanaugh pinned her down, attempted to remove her clothing, held his hand over her mouth when she tried to scream for help and, as she believes it, attempted to rape her.[40]

---

[40]https://www.washingtonpost.com/investigations/california-professor-writer-of-confidential-brett-kavanaugh-letter-speaks-out-about-her-allegation-of-sexual-assault/2018/09/16/46982194-b846-11e8-94eb-3bd52dfe917b_story.html?noredirect=on&utm_term=.fc4f14aa07d4

When these allegations of sexual misconduct were made public, it was clear that Judge Kavanaugh as well as the Republican senators on the Judiciary Committee were caught off guard. When it was revealed that these charges had been known possibility as early as July 6, and certainly known by July 30 by Sen. Dianne Feinstein (Democrat from California) who was sitting on the Judiciary Committee, yet nothing was brought to the Committee for investigation, it looked like a deliberately planned ambush to derail the confirmation process.[41]

Dr. Ford had apparently asked Senator Dianne Feinstein to keep the charges confidential, but they were leaked by someone to the Washington Post. We need to see enough of the details of the allegations to understand why these accusations caused such a media fire storm, triumphant glee in those opposing the confirmation, but consternation to Republicans on the Judiciary Committee, the Judge, and his supporters.

The full allegations that showed up in the Washington Post on September 16 were according to Axios as follows:

> Ford claims that during a house party one summer— she believes it was 1982, when she was 15 and Kavanaugh was 17— Kavanaugh and one of his friends corralled her into a bedroom, where he allegedly pinned her down, groped her, and clumsily attempted to pull off her clothes while intoxicated.
>
> Ford said when she tried to scream, Kavanaugh put his hand over her mouth: "I thought he might inadvertently kill me," she told the Post. "He was trying to attack me and remove my clothing."
>
> She said she was able to escape when Kavanaugh's friend jumped on top of them and knocked them all to the floor.
>
> Ford didn't tell anyone about the incident in any detail until 2012, when she discussed it during a visit to a couples'

---

[41]https://www.axios.com/brett-kavanaugh-timeline-allegations-vote-412d33d6-e5dd-43eb-9322-fd2a3867be9b.html

therapist with her husband. Portions of the therapist's notes were reviewed by the Post, and show Ford described being attacked by boys from an elite private school, though she does not mention Kavanaugh by name.[42]

On Sept. 17, Kavanaugh issued a statement denying Ford's allegations:

"This is a completely false allegation. I have never done anything like what the accuser describes—to her or to anyone."

"Because this never happened, I had no idea who was making this accusation until she identified herself yesterday."

"I am willing to talk to the Senate Judiciary Committee in any way the Committee deems appropriate to refute this false allegation, from 36 years ago, and defend my integrity."

— Brett Kavanaugh[43]

The Response from the Republicans on the Judiciary Committee

The Republicans on the Senate Judiciary Committee rightly called into question the way the Democrats, especially Senator Feinstein of California, had hidden the evidence until the eleventh hour at the close of the investigative process. In no way did they dismiss or ignore the charges brought by Dr. Ford against Judge Kavanaugh, but instead honored her wish to respect her privacy by offering to send a team to California to interview her. While the summary below is out of time sequence as it took place on the day of September 27th, it clearly raises questions about the conduct

---

[42]https://www.axios.com/brett-kavanaugh-sexual-assault-accuser-christine-blasey-ford-dd51d886-ed72-47dc-96f3-e07ef8e838bc.html

[43]https://www.thedailybeast.com/kavanaugh-sexual-assault-accusations-completely-false

and integrity of the Democrats. It is important to view the summary to demonstrate the due diligence of the Republicans to seriously assess the allegations made by Dr. Ford. At the same time, it suggests that the Democrats were conniving to block the confirmation by any means possible.

GRASSLEY (Charles Ernest "Chuck" Grassley is the senior United States Senator from Iowa[R], Senate Judiciary Chairman): Both Dr. Ford and Judge Kavanaugh have been through a terrible couple weeks. They and their families have received vile threats. What they have endured ought to be considered by all of us as unacceptable and a poor reflection on the state of civility in our democracy.

So I want to apologize to you both for the way you've been treated. And I intend, hopefully, for today's hearing to be safe, comfortable and dignified for both of our witnesses. I hope my colleagues will join me in this effort of a show of civility.

With that said, I lament that this hearing — how this hearing has come about...

GRASSLEY: As part of Judge Kavanaugh's nomination to the Supreme Court, the FBI conducted its sixth full field background investigation of Judge Kavanaugh since 1993, 25 years ago. Nowhere in any of these six FBI reports, which committee investigators have reviewed on a bipartisan basis, was there a whiff of any issue—any issue at all related in any way to inappropriate sexual behavior.

Dr. Ford first raised her allegations in a secret letter to the ranking member nearly two months ago in July. This letter was secret from July 30th, September 13th to — no, July 30th until September 13th when I first heard about it.

The ranking member took no action. The letter wasn't shared with me or colleagues or my staff. These allegations could have been investigated in a way that maintained the confidentiality that Dr. Ford requested.

Before his hearing, Judge Kavanaugh met privately with 65 senators, including the ranking member. But the ranking member didn't ask Judge Kavanaugh about the allegations when she met with him privately in August.

The Senate Judiciary Committee held its four-day public hearing from September 4th to September 7th. Judge Kavanaugh testified for more than 32 hours in public. We held a closed session for members to ask sensitive on that—on the last evening, which the ranking member did not attend.

Judge Kavanaugh answered nearly 1,300 written questions submitted by senators after the hearing, more than all prior Supreme Court nominees.

Throughout this period, we did not know about the ranking member's secret evidence. Then, only at an 11th hour, on the eve of Judge Kavanaugh's confirmation vote, did the ranking member refer the allegations to the FBI. And then, sadly, the allegations were leaked to the press. And that's where Dr. Ford was mistreated.

This is a shameful way to treat our witness, who insisted on confidentiality, and—and, of course, Judge Kavanaugh, who has had to address these allegations in the midst of a media circus.

When I received Dr. Ford's letter on September the 13th, my staff and I recognized the seriousness of these allegations and immediately began our committee's investigation, consistent with the way the committee has handled such allegations in the past.

Every step of the way the Democratic side refused to participate in what should have been a bipartisan investigation. And as far as I know on all of our judgeships throughout at least the last four years—or three years, that's been the way it's been handled.

After Dr. Ford's identity became public, my staff contacted all the individuals she said attended the 1982 party described in the Washington Post article.

Judge Kavanaugh immediately submitted to an interview under penalty of felony for any knowingly false statements. He denied the allegations categorically...

GRASSLEY: Democratic staff was invited to participate and could have asked any questions they wanted to, but they declined. Which leads me then to wonder: If they're really concerned with going to the truth, why wouldn't you want to talk to the accused?

The process and procedure is what the committee always does when we receive allegations of wrongdoing.

My staff reached out to other individuals allegedly at the party: Mark Judge, Patrick Smyth, Leland Keyser. All three submitted statements to the Senate under—under penalty of felony—denying any knowledge of the events described by Dr. Ford.

Dr. Ford's lifelong friend, Dr. — Miss Keyser, stated she doesn't know Judge Kavanaugh and doesn't recall ever attending a party with him.

My staff made repeated requests to interview Dr. Ford during the past 11 days, even volunteering to fly to California to take her testimony, but her attorneys refused to prevent — present her allegations to Congress. I never — I nevertheless honored her request for a public hearing, so Dr. Ford today has the opportunity to prevent (sic) her allegations under oath.

As you can see, the Judiciary Committee was able to conduct thorough investigations into allegation — thorough investigations into allegations. . .[44]

This summary clearly reveals Satan's strategies and the human tactics involved for destroying Brett Kavanaugh and blocking his confirmation by any means possible. It was later exposed that Dr. Ford was never told of these offers by the committee to send staff to California to meet with her in private.

More Allegations Exposed by the Press

The Washington Post exposé was followed by other allegations in the New Yorker on the 24th of September. These came out the

---

[44]https://https.www.washingtonpost.com/news/national/wp/2018/09/27kavanaugh -hearing-transcript/?noredirect=on&utm_term.2aed617b4f9c

same day as the Fox News interview.

The second accuser, Deborah Ramirez, claimed that Kavanaugh waved his penis in front of her face while she was inebriated at a dormitory party during the 1983-1984 academic school year. She told Farrow and Mayer that she believed an FBI investigation of Kavanaugh's actions was warranted.

The report alleges that Senate Republicans tried to rush Kavanaugh's nomination to a vote after senior Republican staffers became aware of Ramirez's allegations.

The report also includes quotes from Elizabeth Rasor, a former girlfriend of Mark Judge, who was in the room during Christine Blasey Ford's alleged account of sexual assault by Kavanaugh: "Rasor recalled that Judge had told her ashamedly of an incident that involved him and other boys taking turns having sex with a drunk woman. Rasor said that Judge seemed to regard it as fully consensual."[45]

On September 24, Judge Brett Kavanaugh and his wife, Ashley, were interviewed by Martha MacCallum on Fox News.[46] As I watched this interview, I observed a man reeling from what he emphatically asserted were false charges destroying his lifetime of integrity. You need to see this video to fully grasp the authenticity of Brett and his wife and their struggle to deal with this surprise attack against them[47] that struck the depths of their souls. While on national television with his wife beside him, he had to answer allegations of the most degrading immoral sexual behaviors. This is just one part of the transcript that demonstrates how personal the interview became:

---

[45]https://www.axios.com/brett-kavanaugh-second-accuser-ronan-farrow-34c2f776-27ba-47bc-b008-2ef3e4e5fc2a.html

[46]https://www.realclearpolitics.com/video/2018/09/24/full_interview_judge _kavanaugh_wife_speak_to_fncs_martha_maccallum_about_sexual _allegations.html

[47]The video of the 2018/09/24 interview with Judge Kavanaugh and his wife Ashely. https://youtube/gxEGNt5EwGo

MACCALLUM: ...Did you ever participate in or were you ever aware of any gang-rape that happened at a party that you attended?

B. KAVANAUGH: That's totally false and outrageous. I've never done any such thing, known about any such thing.

When I was in high school—and I went to an all-boys Catholic high school, a Jesuit high school—where I was focused on academics and athletics, going to church every Sunday at Little Flower, working on my service projects, and friendship, friendship with my fellow classmates and friendship with girls from the local all-girls Catholic schools.

And yes, there were parties. And the drinking age was 18, and yes, the seniors were legal and had beer there. And yes, people might have had too many beers on occasion. And people generally in high school—I think all of us have probably done things we look back on in high school and regret or cringe a bit, but that's not what we're talking about. We're talking about an allegation of sexual assault. I've never sexually assaulted anyone. I did not have sexual intercourse or anything close to sexual intercourse in high school or for many years thereafter. And the girls from the schools I went to and I were friends...

MACCALLUM: So, you're saying that through all these years that are in question you were a virgin?

B. KAVANAUGH: That's correct.

MACCALLUM: Never had sexual intercourse with anyone in high school?

B. KAVANAUGH: Correct.

MACCALLUM: and through what years in college since we're probing into your personal life here?

B. KAVANAUGH: Many years after. I'll leave it at that. Many years after. And the people I went to high school with, the girls and the boys, now men and women, that I went to high school with, you know, I was good friends with them and we remain good friends. That's how 65 people on a moment's notice—65 women—220 people total, men and women who knew me in high school.[48] [Kavanaugh is referring to the letters sent by high school and college classmates and those he worked with in the Bush administration who attested to his good character and to his honorable treatment of women.[49]]

I witnessed a godly man, not a perfect man, a devout Roman Catholic being accused of sins he had spent a lifetime by God's grace avoiding. The Holy Spirit came upon me in great power, deepening my own prayer engagement for protecting the Kavanaugh family, but also for protecting the confirmation process.

As I prayed about all this and struggled to assess whether these charges were true or not, I was frankly doubtful. They seemed so out of character for the man with an impeccable record and sterling character.

Furthermore, it all seemed like a well-orchestrated strategy of Satan, the Democrats, and the opposition media to derail and delay the confirmation process. This was noted by Martha MacCallum on the Fox interview: "So, you've got this sort of attempt to kind of swarm a number of people who are putting at least enough doubt out there so that this process will be stymied so that it will take longer, and so that they will get the investigation that they're looking for." Yes, a swarm! Like a lynch mob being stirred up by the media who endlessly reiterate the charges, which even though unproven and uncollaborated, take on the weight of proven facts.

In response to all this, on September 26 Kavanaugh released his

---

[48]https://www.realclearpolitics.com/video/2018/09/24/full_interview_judge_k avanaugh_wife_speak_to_fncs_martha_maccallum_about_sexual_allegations. html

[49]http://www1.cbn.com/cbnnews/politics/2018/september/65-women-come-to-kavanaughs-defense-after-feinstein-reveals-secret-letter-alleging-sexual-isconduct

1982 summer calendars as a way to dispute Ford's timeline.[50]

They were filled with careful notations showing all his activities, mostly having to do with sports, as well as listing by name whom he spent time with.

That same day, a third accuser came forward in a tweet to Attorney Michael Avenatti.[51] He released a sworn declaration from his client, Julie Swetnick, who said Kavanaugh targeted girls for sexual assault. These allegations were even more explicit and outrageous than the first one.

Swetnick alleged that Kavanaugh and his friends would spike drinks with drugs to make girls more vulnerable to sexual assault. She also said Kavanaugh was present when she was gang raped at a party. "They would line up outside rooms at many of these parties waiting for their 'turn' with a girl inside the room."[52]

These charges that were brought were prefaced with demands that the proceedings be delayed and that further FBI investigations be required. The following is from Michael Avenatti, apparently sent to the Judiciary Committee, and also made public:

"Below is my correspondence to Mr. Davis of moments ago, together with a sworn declaration from my client. We demand an immediate FBI investigation into the allegations. Under no circumstances should Brett Kavanaugh be confirmed absent a full and complete investigation.[53]

While Dr. Ford's testimony had some ring of truth and feasibility, these reports were becoming so outrageous that they suggested that Satan and those seeking to block the confirmation were overplaying their hand. Their motivation was exposed in the

---

[50]https://www.axios.com/read-brett-kavanaugh-summer-1982-calendar-b9997863-0edb-4ddc-89f7-d17f328617b9.html

[51]https://www.cbsnews.com/news/michael-avenatti-stormy-daniels-lawyer/

[52]https://twitter.com/MichaelAvenatti/status/1044960428730843136

[53]https://twitter.com/MichaelAvenatti/status/1044960428730843136

repeated demands for more investigations with the obvious intent to cause more delays.

These accusations, including those of Dr. Ford, were all uncorroborated even by the witnesses named. That lack of substantiating evidence, however, did not deter most of the liberal media from assuming that Kavanaugh was guilty of all the charges. Additionally, the reports were picked up by protestors and the internet, who in unison changed their slogans on their printed and hand drawn signs from a focus on abortion rights to: "Believe Women," "Believe Survivors," "We Believe All Survivors," "Kavanaugh Serial Lier, Serial Abuser" etc.[54] It was as if some invisible hand was orchestrating the entire show. It also appeared, but I could not confirm it at that point, that just as Satan finds ground in unhealed hurts, he and his operatives were exploiting the wounding that some of those protesters had experienced. These were impressions I received from the vivid images I saw on the internet and the news.

To these new charges, Brett Kavanaugh and the White House issued the following statements:[55]

A statement from Kavanaugh:

"This alleged event from 35 years ago did not happen. The people who knew me then know that this did not happen, and have said so. This is a smear, plain and simple. I look forward to testifying on Thursday about the truth, and defending my good name—and the reputation for character and integrity I have spent a lifetime building—against these last-minute allegations."

---

[54]You can see these in the many pictures on the internet of the protesters.

[55]https://www.axios.com/brett-kavanaugh-second-accuser-ronan-farrow-34c2f776-27ba-47bc-b008-2ef3e4e5fc2a.html

A statement from White House spokesperson Kerri Kupec:

"This 35-year-old, uncorroborated claim is the latest in a coordinated smear campaign by the Democrats designed to tear down a good man. This claim is denied by all who were said to be present and is wholly inconsistent with what many women and men who knew Judge Kavanaugh at the time in college say. The White House stands firmly behind Judge Kavanaugh."

The strategy of the Democrats became clear in a letter from Senator Dianne Feinstein to Senate Judiciary Chairman Chuck Grassley:

"I am writing to request an immediate postponement of any further proceedings related to the nomination of Brett Kavanaugh. I also ask that the newest allegations of sexual misconduct be referred to the FBI for investigation, and that you join our request for the White House to direct the FBI to investigate the allegations of Christine Blasey Ford as well as these new claims."[56]

The tactic was to delay the proceedings related to the nomination for as long as possible by every means possible. As I heard these allegations and denials and struggled to understand what was really going on, my prayer was: **"Lord, pierce the cloaking and expose what is really true about these charges. Lord, expose what Satan's plans are in all of this!"**

After the surprise attack of the allegations by Dr. Ford, followed by the cascade of more and more graphic charges brought against Kavanaugh, there was a noticeable change of tone in the press and among the Democrats on the Judiciary Committee. From my perspective, it seemed like orchestrated confusion that had an

---

[56]https://www.axios.com/brett-kavanaugh-second-accuser-ronan-farrow-34c2f776-27ba-47bc-b008-2ef3e4e5fc2a.html

unrestrained, dangerous, and irrational tone. Judge Kavanaugh and his supporters seemed under assault by a frenzied, irrational mob whose one aim was to destroy not just his confirmation, but the man himself, by denying him any due process or the assumption of innocence until proven guilty.

During those days I slept fitfully, continually praying in tongues. When I did sleep, I experienced restless dreams where I was hounded by evil spirits, who like a pack of ravenous wolves seemed to be closing in for the kill on Judge Kavanaugh and his appointment. I intensely felt I was doing battle with very high-level demonic spirits of lawlessness and destruction who were working to destroy our rational democratic processes in order to impose tyranny. In this battle, I was functioning in the name and authority of Jesus Christ, with the Sword of the Spirit in hand.

At times the demons would turn on me causing mental confusion and visceral reactions of nausea and fear. When these attacks came, the tongues would shift to singing in the Spirit. I knew the Lord was providing a shield around me to pray without ceasing.

During this phase of the battle, the intercessors were in constant communication with each other through email, text messaging, and phone calls. We were sharing information, prophetic words, and words of knowledge that we were getting from the Lord. In the spiritual realm, there seemed to be a gathering of demonic and angelic forces hurtling toward a major clash. We did not know when this clash would take place, but we suspected it might happen on the 27th when Dr. Christine Ford and Judge Brett Kavanaugh were to appear before the Judiciary Committee. On that day, Dr. Ford, accompanied by her lawyers, was to bring her allegations against Judge Kavanaugh. The Republican senators on the Committee hired sex crime prosecutor Rachel Mitchell to question both Dr. Ford and Judge Kavanaugh. The hearings were to be televised to the nation.

The Holy Spirit Calls the Prayer Cohort

Leading up to the 27th, Jesus our Commander in Chief was working to form us into a prayer cohort. The role of a prayer cohort in the realm of the spirit is equivalent to a police SWAT team deployed into situations of great danger. A prayer cohort requires special training, spiritual weapons, authorization from Jesus, and the anointing of the Holy Spirit. The Lord often gathers the cohort members out of a network of intercessors who are already connected in prayer together. Such a cohort was needed for the upcoming battle to engage with high-level demonic entities who were orchestrating the human and demonic clashes about to take place.

Dealing with high-level demonic spirits requires special equipping and anointing by the Holy Spirit. If these demons are engaged without the anointing, equipping, and authorization of Jesus Christ, they can inflict significant, and possibility fatal spiritual, physical and emotional harm. Even with the full covering of Jesus and His calling, there can be serious counter attacks against the intercessors, their families, or the ministry they are associated with.

The Lord was well ahead of us in planning for this battle. It turned out that a year before the Kavanagh nomination, PRMI had scheduled our Dunamis Project Equipping Event on Listening Evangelism the same week of the 27th when the hearing between Dr. Ford and Judge Kavanaugh were to take place. A few months before this event, a fire at PRMI's Community of the Cross destroyed our meeting rooms. As a result, the venue had to be moved a few miles away to the Baptists' Ridgecrest Conference Center.

This change of venue had some consequences, which in retrospect seemed part of God's preparation for the cohort He was gathering for the battle on September 27th. First, because of the cost connected to the venue, our number of participants was greatly reduced. This gave us more flexibility in adapting members of the team to be called into the engagement. We were also in the context of a large evangelical community of believers. There were many African and Spanish American congregations having church conferences at the same venue. The entire conference complex felt centered in Jesus Christ, whose name was on hundreds of lips in word and praise. One other advantage of Ridgecrest is that it afforded a lookout place at a higher altitude than the one at the Community of the Cross, the site where I was to be called to engage high-level demons.

In addition to the geographical location, the Lord had called a team of well-equipped and anointed intercessors to provide prayer cover for the scheduled equipping event. They were the very ones whom the Lord called to form the cohort to engage in this battle. Also, there were forty participants in the equipping event who provided backup cover of worship and prayer.

The cohort consisted of a team of seasoned, anointed intercessors, all of whom had extensive experience in this type of high-level prayer and spiritual warfare. We were also supported online by off-site intercessors from the USA, the UK, and Canada.

We all knew each other well. Being in many engagements over the years with high-level demonic powers as a "band of brothers and sisters," we had formed deep bonds of love and trust together. We also had learned to appreciate how the Lord worked uniquely through each of us. We were fully aware of one another's personality quirks and foibles, as well as each other's gifts and strengths.

The core team on site included Jon and Joan Gurley, JuleAnn Martin, Martha Earley, and Lauren Rittman. Jon Gurley constantly assessed news services and prophetic ministries over the internet, and listened to the Holy Spirit to provide intelligence. The Rev. Cindy Strickler, Director of PRMI and the Dunamis Fellowship, provided spiritual cover for the entire equipping event as well as for the cohort. For me personally, she functioned very much in the Aaron role of providing support.

Off-site intercessors also provided the cohort with spiritual backing and intelligence. The Rev. Martin Boardman from England, but now living in Canada, serves as the PRMI Prayer Mobilizer. He constantly connected with the PRMI prayer networks. Someone gifted in prophetic discernment was Kim Krog in New York. There were several intercessors in Canada, one being a Christian Reformed pastor who asked not to be named, but played a key role in this battle. A very important member of the team was Pauline Eyles, a PRMI Board member from England who represented the spiritual cover provided by the PRMI International Board of Directors. The POTUS/SCOTUS WhatsApp group were also extremely active. This American group consisted of experienced and anointed intercessors with a special burden to pray for President Trump and his nomination of judges to the Supreme Court. The complete PRMI off-site prayer network consists of about 50 people, but for this battle God just mobilized a few: Barb Koob, Celia Warner, Diane Bosley, Kayse Dean, Kim Krog and one other person who was on site at Ridgecrest. Roy and Betsy Washburn with Intercessors for America were providing off-site insights from the perspective of IFA who were holding a prayer vigil near the location of the hearings throughout the entire confirmation battle.[57]

Each team member was personally drawn into this battle and played a unique role. For example, JuleAnn reported the following as a lead-up to the decisive battle of the 27th.

The Buildup to the Second Engagement as Experienced by an Intercessor

JuleAnn wrote the following personal note recounting how the Holy Spirit gave her guidance, and how she experienced demonic attack in the lead-up to the battle on the 27th. She resides in the Northeast USA.

"During the thick of the controversy, Fox News interviewed

---

[57]For more on the prayer mobilization by Intercessors for America, go to: https://www.prayerrequest.com/threads/an-urgent-message-from-intercessors-for-america.4070698/

Brett Kavanaugh and his wife. Once again, I had felt the burden of intercession to pray protection for this family. For weeks Holy Spirit would wake me at night to pray for the situation as I watched each day on the news the manifestation of rage, hatred, murder, and seeing how irrational people were acting. I felt like I was watching people lose all sense of reality. I was in prayer almost constantly."

"Sometime during these weeks of engagement, I received a message from the Director of the event, asking if I would lead intercession for the Dunamis Project Unit 6 on evangelism in Black Mountain. Strangely, this email went into my junk mail and I didn't see it until his wife contacted me through Face Book Messenger. I asked the LORD that if He wanted me to go, He would have to have everything prearranged for me to have a means to get there and a place to stay.

"Prior to leaving for NC, there had been some sort of satanic ritual done in my back yard to curse us. A deer had been slaughtered and its blood sprinkled all over the back yard. Also, cat urine had been poured around the back of the house. Katie, my 31-year-old daughter and I broke the curse against us. Both Katie and I had been suffering from headaches—I had been in bed for two days—and these headaches were relieved after the curse was broken in the name of Jesus Christ.

"I was joined on the 13-hour drive down to Black Mountain by The Rev. Trevor Payton, the Executive Director of Dunamis Fellowship Canada. In the car, we had deep conversation about the circumstances of Canada and the United States and the connection of Far-left and Islam and the danger to the Western Judeo-Christian form of government. We also moved into prayer and worship as the miles sped by. It was glorious, and felt like angels were with us in the car. For me it was very important to have Rev. Trever Peyton with us. He is a man of great spiritual authority, teaching gifts, and also represents the Canadian expression of this movement of the Holy Spirit. In this battle to uphold Judeo-Christian values, it is so important that we have the Canadian and British part of the ministry involved. We are really in this together!

"When we arrived in Black Mountain, NC, I talked to Martha at length about this intercessory engagement and the burden I had been feeling for weeks. The night before the engagement I had a very strong sense that the next day would be a major engagement. I could sense things building. I shared that with Martha and asked her if she could step in and take my position as point person for intercessory prayer. She agreed. Holy Spirit woke me up during that night about 2:30/3:00 as usual and as I prayed, I seemed to hear Him say, "It is time to bring out the battering-ram." Then I saw this triangular tube thing with a giant steel pointed pole in the center. As I prayed about it, I knew the engagement was coming. When the engagement did happen the next morning, I was not surprised."

Before rushing to describe the amazing prayer battle that took place the next day, let us pause and do an After-Action Review. There are some very important lessons to be learned in this build-up process that took place prior to the clash in the heavenlies.

5

Second Engagement: Phase 1–After-Action Review: Preparing the Cohort for the Second Engagement

This chapter offers an after-action review of the first part of the second engagement. The prayer team was so tired from the time of prayer intercession and the work of preparing for the conference, that we did not pause for an after-action review following the first preparatory phase of the engagement. Instead, we rushed into the ferocious prayer battle of September 27th. In retrospect, we would have been better prepared for the upcoming battle if we had conducted an after-action review.

Various Units in the Army of Intercessors[58]

One of the timeless lessons I learned from this and other high-level prayer battles is the strategic role of the prayer cohort in God's battle plan. Therefore, before we move into the high-level engagement of September 27, it is important that we explain the nature of the prayer cohort the Lord was forming us into.

A prayer cohort must be understood within the larger context of God's army of intercessors. This army is made up of many different units.   The largest grouping is the pervasive on-going work of the Holy Spirit praying through all those of biblical faith. This includes the prayers of Jews and Christians crying out to the One True God revealed in the Old and New Testaments. This general work of prayer is expressed specifically in the Jewish Amidah[59], "You are eternally mighty, Lord. You give life to the dead and have great power to save..."[60]   It is also embodied in Yeshua/Jesus' direction that we pray, "...may your kingdom come, may your will be done on earth as it is in heaven." (Matthew 6:10-11) The general and pervasive work of prayer may also include the prayers of those whom the Bible identifies as those who "fear God" and follow the dictates of the conscience and show that the "work

---

[58]In what follows I have adapted from Chapter 3 "Cohorts of Intercessors" from my book *A Prayer Strategy for the Victory of Jesus Christ: Defeating the Demonic Strongholds of ISIS and Radical Islam* by Zeb Bradford Long, Exousia Press, (2016) www.prmi.org

[59] The Amidah (Hebrew: תפילת העמידה, Tefilat HaAmidah, "The Standing Prayer"), also called the Shemoneh Esreh (שמנה עשרה), is the central prayer of the Jewish liturgy. This prayer, among others, is found in the siddur, the traditional Jewish prayer book. Due to its importance, it is simply called hatefila (תפילה, "prayer") in rabbinic literature. [1]
https://en.wikipedia.org/wiki/Amidah

[60]*The Koren Siddur*, Korn Publishers Jerusalem, Orthodox Union 2013, p. 480.

of the Torah is written in their hearts." (Romans 2:14-16 TLV)[61] This could include those of many different faiths and of no formal religious faith.

The general work of prayer is also taking place as the Holy Spirit indwells all those who are born again into the Kingdom of God and have the Holy Spirit both dwelling in them and praying through them:

> In the same way, the Spirit helps us in our weakness, for we do not know how we should pray, but the Spirit himself intercedes for us with inexpressible groanings.27And he who searches our hearts knows the mind of the Spirit, because the Spirit intercedes on behalf of the saints according to God's will. (Romans 8:26-27)

The intercession of the Holy Spirit through every Christian, whether individually or gathered in prayer groups, enables a general work of prayer and faith that facilitates the presence and working of God the Father, Son, and Holy Spirit among people and throughout history.

From this pervasive prayer, the Lord has conducted all through history what may be identified as "concerts of prayer." These arise from waves or pulses of the Holy Spirit through which the Kingdom of God is advanced, and the Great Commission is fulfilled. Examples are the prayer movements that preceded the great outpouring of the Holy Spirit from 1890 to 1910. This included the D.L. Moody and R.A. Torrey revivals in the English-speaking world, the Welsh revival, the Korean revival, and others. A more recent example is the 1960-1980s outpouring of the Holy Spirit in the

---

[61]Romans 2:14-16 TLV For when Gentiles, who do not have the Torah, do by nature the things of the Torah, they are a law to themselves even though they do not have the Torah. (15) They show that the work of the Torah is written in their hearts, their conscience bearing witness and their thoughts switching between accusing or defending them (16) on the day when God judges the secrets of men according to my Good News through Messiah Yeshua.

Charismatic renewal. Such concerts of prayer may also take place as God's response to overcoming threats to His Kingdom from Satan's demonic strongholds.

As I stated in the opening chapter giving the spiritual context of the confirmation battle, I believe that we are presently in another major movement of the Holy Spirit which may be identified as the westward blowing wind of the Spirit that began in Jerusalem with Pentecost and is now returning to Jerusalem.

Pervasive faith and prayer among believers provide Jesus with a global communication network. The Holy Spirit, who is both in heaven, symbolized in the "seven torches of fire burning before the throne" and "sent out into all the earth," makes this network possible. (Revelation 4:5, 5:6) Human means of communication such as the internet and phone calls complement this global spiritual communication system. The general work of prayer is unceasing and pervasive. The Holy Spirit may, like the wind on a lake, stir up a wave of prayer to accomplish a special work. These may be called concerts of prayer and take place during a time of crisis or during periods preparing for outpourings of the Holy Spirit to advance the Kingdom of God.

In addition to this pervasive work of prayer is intercessory prayer that takes place in gathered communities for the ongoing work of prayer to sustain the advancement of the Kingdom of God. The Roman Catholic and Orthodox streams of Christianity are replete with examples. In these traditions, monasteries and convents have practiced prayer for centuries. Within the Protestant stream, the Holy Spirit raised up many prayer centers to sustain the work of missions. One famous example is the 100-year prayer meeting that grew out of the Moravian revival of 1727.[62] The result of this extended period of extraordinary prayer is a global missionary movement which has brought many thousands into the Kingdom of God.

Since the 1960's outpouring of the Holy Spirit in the

---

[62]"Moravian Revival," Jul. 6, 2005, by Evan Wiggs. http://www.evanwiggs.com/revival/history/moravian.html.

Charismatic and Third Wave movements, many places of focused, continuous prayer have appeared. One is Jesus Abbey in South Korea, which has sustained the rhythms of prayer on the Benedictine model since its founding by Archer Torrey in 1965.[63] Another is the International House of Prayer in Kansas City which has maintained 24/7 prayer for years. They have become a university to equip disciples of Jesus Christ within the context of this on-going life of prayer.[64] Yet another location is the Jerusalem Prayer Tower overlooking the Old City of Jerusalem which welcomes people from all nations to come and pray.[65] This is a unique prayer center that represents the move of the Holy Spirit in bringing Jews to faith in Messiah Jesus, in fulfillment of the restoration of Israel, as found in Romans 11.

In addition to these set apart places of prayer are ones which have grown up around PRMI over many years. Their spiritual centering point is the Community of the Cross, PRMI's prayer equipping and sending center located in the mountains of western North Carolina.

The gift the internet has brought to this Kingdom work of intercession is that these prayer centers no longer need to be confined to geographic space. Many are located in "cyberspace" with networks of intercessors who may span the globe.

There were two "cyberspace" prayer networks that were especially called to the battle of appointing originalist judges to the US Supreme Court. These were POTUS Shield

---

[63]Jesus Abbey's website, http://www.jabbey.org/bbs/main.php.

"Jesus Abbey's Three Seas Center," Jesus Abbey, http://www.the fourthriver.org/PDF%20Documents/Main%20Brochure%20English.pdf.

[64]The International House of Prayer (IHOP) was started on May 7, 1999 by Mike Bickle. http://www.ihopkc.org/ihopu/

[65]Jerusalem Prayer Tower, http://www.jerusalemprayertower.org/
Originally uploaded on en.wikipedia by Paul Barlow. (Transferred by lux2545) public domain.

(https://www.potusshield.org/) and Intercessors for America (https://www.ifapray.org/). Another group was the Capitol Hill Prayer Partners (chpponline.blogspot.com). We had no personal association with this group, but their "Daily Brief" emails sent throughout the confirmation battle were filled with up-to-date information of the events taking place, as well as reliable discernment of the spiritual dynamics and guidance of how to pray effectively.[66] These networks were primarily based on the internet, but people also gathered in special focus prayer work at strategic locations. For example, in addition to their cyberspace prayer network, a prayer team representing Intercessors for America gathered on site in Washington, DC during the Kavanaugh hearings. PRMI's prayer work was part of the much larger global concert of prayer taking place among these centers and networks of intercession. While we did communicate with each other, the governing and coordinating authority for this prayer work was the Holy Spirit.

The Prayer Cohort as the Vanguard of God's Prayer Army

Drawn from PRMI's network of intercessors was a special team called a "prayer cohort." A cohort consists of a key number of intercessors—we have found the optimal number to be seven— who are formed into a cohesive team. These are people called, equipped, and anointed for engagements against the demonic powers behind human structures of evil.

The story of Moses, Aaron and Hur praying on the mountain as recorded in Exodus 17:8-16 serves as a template for how the Holy Spirit prepares us for battle through the formation of prayer cohorts. It is helpful to understand the different roles various intercessors played within the major engagement in the

---

[66]Capitol Hill Prayer Partners
https://www.blogger.com/profile/14025235394365544163

heavenlies. Moses, Aaron and Hur on the mountain demonstrate the three most basic roles needed within a cohort for it to effectively cooperate with the Holy Spirit in intercession and engagements with high-level demons. In practice these roles are fluid, and may be shared by different people depending on the calling and anointing of the Holy Spirit.

The English pre-Raphaelite artist Millais painted Moses, Aaron, and Hur during the battle of Rephidim against the Amalekites. He vividly portrayed the model of a cohort of intercessors in action.[67] Mallais's artistic interpretation may help us learn the following dynamics and roles of an effective prayer team:

The Moses Role as the Visionary Leader

The first role necessary in a prayer cohort is that of a visionary leader. The work of intercession is to be the go-between in the spiritual and human realms so that the plans of God are fulfilled. This role of an intercessor as visionary leader is placed on someone who has been given a glimpse of the blue print of God's plans and is called to pray it into reality. In the battle of Amalek, Moses is given the role of visionary leader and called to stand in the gap as intercessor. Often a prayer cohort will form around the person in the visionary intercessor role.

Victory O Lord by John Everett Millais (1829–1896)

---

[67]*Victory O Lord!* (1871) by John Everett Millais (1829–1896)
https://commons.wikimedia.org/w/index.php?curid=18811161

In the Kavanaugh prayer battle, I was called to take the Moses role as visionary leader. I was, however, joined by JuleAnn who also functioned very much in the Moses visionary leader role in the three engagements that took place. The Holy Spirit gave us both guidance to step into the gap and be in the frontline of the battle.

The Role of Aaron Embodies Love and Friendship While Upholding Moses, the Intercessor.

In the left of the Millais painting, Aaron is shown leaning into Moses and holding up his right arm.   His eyes are directed toward the battle in the valley below, but he is also focused on Moses. There seems to be a close relationship between them. This would be expected as they are brothers and fellow clansman. (Exodus 4:14)[68]

Aaron is the model of all who are called to pray for the ones involved in the actual conflict. They support the Moses-type prayer leader with love, friendship, and protection. As they stand with the leader, they are in the gap and in the battle, but do not function as the point person in leadership.

This critical role is very personal and based on deep spiritual friendship of heart to heart connection. Aaron-type intercessors have provided me with the love and friendship to support me in the lonely prayer battles I have fought. Often, the Holy Spirit notified them to pray for me even before I had a chance to contact them. They often felt within themselves the battles in the spiritual realm and experienced in their own bodies the agonies of earnest prayer or the assaults by demonic spirits. They have served as a shield, providing the space for me to focus entirely on the battle without having to worry about protecting my back.

JuleAnn and I each had several Aaron-type intercessors who

---

[68]For some discussions on this issue of whether Moses and Aaron were blood brothers, see this site. https://thetorah.com/moses-aaron-and-miriam-were-they-siblings/

provided the support of love, friendship, and encouragement to us. Some were with us on site, and others felt they were present with us even though they were thousands of miles from us. In the first draft of the chapter on the second engagement, I listed by name the intercessors whom God had gathered at the Ridgecrest Conference Center. One was Martin Boardman, our PRMI Prayer Coordinator. When he reviewed the chapter, he reminded me that he had not been on site, but at home in Alberta, Canada. I was shocked! I had experienced him so very present in the realm of the Spirit that I thought he had been physically with me. This shows how the brothers and sisters within a prayer cohort are so tightly knit together in the Spirit as to transcend time and space, comparable to the close relationships that form among solders in combat as they are forged into a "band of brothers."[69]

The Role of Hur Provides Strength and Actionable Intelligence to Support the Intercessor

The third figure in the Millais painting is Hur holding up Moses' left arm. Notice Hur's strong, muscular arm and his erect, steel-like posture, standing immovable in the spiritual battle. His will is set on upholding Moses' arm with all his massive strength until the victory is won.

Hur seems to be looking outward over the battle. Perhaps his gaze extends all the way to the Promised Land where he sees the fulfillment of God's plan in directing His people there through the strategic victory of the battle below him. I know this reflects artistic imagination more than biblical revelation. But Hur may be a type of intercessor who stands firm in his faith in Jesus Christ. When I am in the thick of a prayer battle, it is very easy to get overwhelmed and confused about who has the victory. Many times, God has

---

[69] I get this term from the book and TV miniseries, "Band of Brothers," a 2001 American war drama miniseries based on historian Stephen E. Ambrose's 1992 non-fiction book *Band of Brothers*.
https://en.wikipedia.org/wiki/Band_of_Brothers_(miniseries)

upheld me through another intercessor's steadfast faith and authority in Jesus Christ. They have also joined in the fight by receiving guidance from the Holy Spirit as to the ebb and flow of the battle and how God is directing me to pray. Other times, Hur-type intercessors have served as intelligence officers who listen to the Holy Spirit while assessing news reports and gathering and analyzing information. Any guidance they receive is passed on to the visionary leader.

There were several intercessors gathered at the conference center who functioned in this role. They were constantly on their mobile phones or tablets, checking news outlets and engaged in constant connection with other intercessors to receive spiritual intelligence. The most common way guidance is given to intercessors is through words of Scripture highlighted by the Holy Spirit; but prophetic visions and words of knowledge also play an important role. When in the thick of the battle, the visionary leader cannot assess and discern everything from the Lord with such a massive amount of data coming in. Therefore, Hur Intercessors have an extremely important role of working through the intelligence among themselves before passing it on to intercessors on the frontlines of the battle.

The dynamic of Hur-type intercessors passing on guidance from the Holy Spirit to the visionary leader occurs throughout each prayer engagement. The information and suggested guidance need to be discerned by the visionary leader, but the process is made easier when Hur intercessors have distilled the information into what they believe is guidance from the Holy Spirit.

Other Roles in the Cohort

Other roles not included in the Old Testament motif of Moses, Aaron, and Hur are needed for the full functioning of the intercessory cohort. These will be unique to the individuals who are called with their individual spiritual giftings, personalities, and experiences.

One such role is that of networker and communicator. This

person is involved in the prayer work, but is also gifted at including others in the process. This requires good communication skills to grasp the essence of what is going on in the spiritual realm and communicate it to others. The work is often done through internet communication by joining in the discernment process and in actual prayer engagements.

There were several on-site network communicators in the prayer battle surrounding the Kavanaugh hearings. Off site was Rev. Martin Boardman, who is a gifted communicator and networker. Even though he was in Alberta, Canada during these engagements, it seemed that he was sitting in the master command and control center in Jesus' war room. He was constantly listening to the Holy Spirit and simultaneously connecting to and keeping the intercessors connected.

There are many other roles in the cohort, as many as there are personality types and different configurations of spiritual gifting, but these seem to be the main types that are needed by the Holy Spirit to form a cohort. In retrospect, we realized in the weeks leading up to the climactic battle on the 27th, that the Lord was forming us into a cohort needed for the clashes that were to take place. It was possible to form the cohort just in time for the impending strategic Kingdom battles because of the extensive equipping and experience the PRMI intercessors had already had.

Let us return to the battlespace to see how the Lord used our various intercessory roles in an extraordinary engagement in the spiritual realm, one that interfaced with political/cultural clashes during the hearings conducted by the Senate Judiciary Committee.

Chapter 5 After Action Review: Gathering the Cohort

6

Second Engagement: Phase 2—The Clash in the Heavenlies

The clash came on September 27, the day Brett Kavanaugh's accuser Dr. Christine Ford was to bring testimony to the Senate Judiciary Committee. Dr. Ford was scheduled to present in the morning, and Brett Kavanaugh in the afternoon. In retrospect, this was a decisive power encounter in the heavenlies for the fulfillment of God's plan for Judge Kavanaugh to be confirmed to the Supreme Court. But there was no certainty of this outcome at the time. The fog of war was so thick—we were going forward moment by moment in obedience to the guidance of the Holy Spirit. It was only during the After-Action Review that followed that we were able to reconstruct the way the Holy Spirit guided us in this battle.

My (Brad's) Call Up the Mountain

I was supposed to teach the entire morning of September 27, and the Senate hearing was scheduled to begin at 10:00 am. As I began teaching, I felt the Holy Spirit falling upon me, calling me out of teaching mode and into the heavenlies for a prayer engagement. At the same time, Jon and Joan Gurley, JuleAnn Martin, and Lauren Rittman were also being called out of the meeting and into prayer.

Just before ten o'clock, the Holy Spirit was almost shouting at me that it was time to stop teaching. He was shifting my anointing from teaching to intercession. Jon, sitting in the back, urgently waved at me and pointed to his watch. I knew I was moving into disobedience if I tried to complete the teaching. So I turned the meeting over to Cindy (PRMI's Director) for oversight, and to Trevor Peyton to pick up the teaching role. The Director of the Dunamis event made an announcement releasing those who were being called into intercession.

The Rev. Cindy Strickler functioned in the role of an Aaron-type intercessor by supporting me in prayer and providing the cover for the Evangelism Dunamis. Jon, Joan, JuleAnn, Martha, Lauren, and others stepped into the gap to engage in the battle and provide cover for me.

The Holy Spirit led me up the mountain behind the conference center. The weather was misty and drizzling, but I knew the Lord was leading me to hike up to the high point called Royal Gorge Overlook. Jon called and asked if I wanted to join them in prayer in a set-apart prayer room. I knew I was called up alone into the battle, so I declined. However, I knew I had their strong prayer covering.

Ridgecrest is a huge sprawling conference center with buildings half way up the valley. As I made my way past the buildings, the Holy Spirit was praying through me in tongues with growing intensity. When I got out of range of the buildings, I started praying aloud in tongues, Chinese, and English and singing in the Spirit.

The strenuous hike of several miles was a time of preparation. The Lord brought to mind my many sins which I confessed out loud in Chinese, just in case I was being overheard. As I got higher and higher up and further away from the buildings and people, I entered into a spiritual and natural wilderness made more ominous by the mist and drizzle where waves of dread swept over me.

For a while I heard noises coming from up above me, and I imagined there were bears following me. As I got even higher up and could not see more than a few yards in front of me, I imagined I was smelling a Bigfoot stalking me with malevolent intent. The fog was contorted by my vivid imagination into whole Bigfoot families after me. (There have actually been reports of such sightings in the area.) I dearly wished I had my 45-caliber pistol with me, but the conference center did not allow concealed carry on their land. So, I prayed all the louder in tongues and shouted into the fog that I belonged to Jesus and that nothing would deter me from my mission.

Those fears lifted for a while. Then Satan shifted his attack. It seemed to grow in intensity as I trudged higher and higher up the steep road. Waves of dread swept over me that I would have a heart attack and die right there, or I would slip into a ravine and break my neck. It felt like evil spirits were after me, reminding me of past sins which had already been forgiven. I became overwhelmed by a feeling of the compete uselessness and utter folly of prayer. Waves of despair washed over me that the battle was already lost. I wondered whether I was going insane to think prayer would make any difference at all. I was struggling with many inner battles. In addition, it started to rain hard. I had left my rain coat at home. My sports jacket was soaked; my Tilly hat was dripping wet. I was sorely tempted to just turn back when my mobile phone rang.

It was John Chang! A great man of prayer who is the anointed leader of PRMI's Chinese work. The Holy Spirit had prompted him to give me a call just at that moment. Praise God! I told him what was happening, and he instantly launched into a prayer in Chinese for my protection and for the anointing of the Holy Spirit to empower me to continue on up the mountain and be faithful in the engagement against powers and principalities. He also promised to mobilize the intercessors at his church to join in praying for my protection and anointing for the battle. Strengthened by his prayer and friendship and knowing that my brother was joining me in the battle, I persisted for another mile up the mountain. The rain turned back to drizzle and the mist started to lift.

Finally, I arrived at the location where I knew the clash awaited me—the lookout overlooking the gorge. It is a raised wooden platform with railings around it. All I could see was a mountain peak above me protruding through the mist, and far below in a clear patch I could see trucks laboring up the steep grade on Interstate 40 East. I called my wife Laura to tell her where I was so she could be praying for me and know where to find me in case this was to be my final battle on earth.

I was up there for a couple of hours. I kept pacing back and forth and praying in the spirit. From time to time, I would stop and have a small cup of hot tea from the thermos Laura had handed me as I had left home. I was so caught up in the Spirit that I was not aware of the time, nor the wet and cold, until much later when the Spirit lifted.

Much happened in phases. Much was visionary and nearly impossible to communicate. But here are some high points.

First, the Holy Spirit prayed through me, surging like a wild river. Most of the time I did not know what He was praying or doing. I just surrendered and let the Spirit pray through me, like it says in Romans 8, with groans too deep for words. Yet, all the time my mind was sharp in processing all the information, and my will was set on following Jesus into whatever He called me.

There were times when I was praying for the protection of Brett Kavanaugh and the Republican senators. I felt like there were bubbles or force fields of protection around them that were being sustained through my prayers and the prayers of others. I was not led at all to pray for the Democratic senators, except that the schemes Satan was working through them would be blocked.

I focused considerable time on praying that Kavanaugh would be anointed by the Holy Spirit to know what and how to speak to defend himself. I did not know it at the time, but those prayers were prayed during the morning when Dr. Christine Ford was presenting, and Brett Kavanaugh was preparing his statements.

There were extended periods when the Holy Spirit called me to bind the high-level demons of anarchy and lawlessness. This battle lasted a long time. Finally, I pushed through until I knew they were defeated. It felt like terrible powers of evil were coming against me, seeking to destroy me. But like fierce rabid dogs, they were held at a distance by unbreakable chains. I was aware of angels protecting me. I felt the love and presence of Jesus Christ and the fellowship of the Aaron intercessors supporting me. Though difficult to describe, I knew I was not alone, but in the great fellowship of all the saints in heaven and still alive on earth, joining hands in this great battle of advancing the Kingdom of God. At one point I had a vivid vision of angels battling demons over the Capital in Washington, DC where the hearing was taking place.

Within the intensity of the battle, the Holy Spirit spoke with perfect clarity that God the Father had called Brett Kavanaugh to the Supreme Court in order to uphold and defend the Judeo-Christian values upon which America was founded. The Holy Spirit told me I was to proclaim this fact to the powers and principalities that were opposing God's will. I shouted out this word over the mountain valley. As I did, I felt in my spirit and saw in my mind's eye, like expanding ripples on a lake, actions being set in motion. These actions resulted in spiritual and human opposition being thrust back, and Judge Kavanaugh being installed on the Supreme Court. I could see Satan's lines of defense being breached and held open just long enough for the decisions to be made for Kavanaugh's nomination to be confirmed by the Judiciary Committee.

The Lord then said this would not take place immediately, but after a short delay in His own good time. But it would happen. The Lord also said it would not take place unless intercessors were obedient and wise bold decisions were made by those on the Judiciary Committee. I was called to pray for a further mobilization of intercessors, as well as for all the Republican senators involved. I was also called to pray for several Democratic senators, that Satan's plan of working through them to block the confirmation would be thwarted.

The Lord said, "You must now move into praise, as praise will unleash my work in the world. You will be joining a great symphony of intercessors and worshipers whom I have called into the gap to fight the battle." As this word was coming, words of praise and thanksgiving were already welling up from the depths of my spirit. I sang and praised Jesus Christ, the Father, and the Holy Spirit in English, Chinese, and in tongues at the top of my voice. This lasted a long time. In my mind's eye I could see demons retreating in terror and demonic strongholds crumbing, liberating their human captives. In vivid biblical images I saw the advancement of the Kingdom of God, the nations of the world streaming into Jerusalem—the City of the Great King, the fulfillment of the Great Commission, and the dawn of the New Heaven and New Earth.

Suddenly the Holy Spirit said, "You are released from this battle. You can start down the mountain." With that word, the Holy Spirit's power lifted from me. Like awakening from a vivid fantastic dream, I was no longer in the heavenlies, but with both feet standing on a wooden platform wet with rain, overlooking a mist shrouded gorge in the Blue Ridge Mountains. But springs of joy and praise continued to well up within me. My spirit was still in the dance of cooperation with the Holy Spirit. It was about 12:30 pm by this time. It took what seemed like forever to make it down the mountain's rocky overgrown path. Finally, I walked into the conference center dining room and was met by relieved intercessors who were very happy to see me alive. I later learned that the intercessors had experienced a terrible battle for my protection in which they physically experienced the rage of Satan directed against me. They had in fact feared for my life. Actually, I had feared this too, except I had been too engaged in the battle to think much about the likelihood that these demonic attacks could be fatal to my physical being.

I was completely exhausted, drenched, and shivering with cold. I ate some lunch as the intercessors told me of the prayer battle they had been through. I, personally, could not share much as I was still caught up in the Spirit. The experience was raw and unformed;

my emotions were in turmoil. The members of the cohort laid hands on me and prayed for me. Then I went home, took a hot shower, and had a cup of hot tea.

I continued in prayer all afternoon and into the evening as I watched the live proceedings of Judge Kavanaugh giving his defense and being questioned by the sex crimes prosecutor Rachel Mitchell and the Democratic and Republican senators. I also watched a replay of the testimony by Dr. Christine Ford, and was impressed with the careful, respectful way Rachel Mitchel questioned her. I prayed in the spirit all night.

The next morning, I woke up physically bruised and battered all over. I was so sore I could hardly walk. This battering resulted in part from the hike up and down the mountain, but more so, from the battle with invisible powers that had pummeled my physical body. I was both emotionally and spiritually exhausted, but also exhilarated and swept up in a hilarious joy of having been called as a co-warrior with the Holy Spirit and the angels in this combat with the Devil.

The Holy Spirit remained on me in power, leading me to continue in prayer until the vote was taken by the Judiciary Committee to approve Brett Kavanaugh's nomination to the Supreme Court.

JuleAnn's Report of the September 27 Engagement

It is important to understand what was happening to the team while I was on the mountain. I knew they were supporting me and felt them with me in the battle, but I really had no idea what they were going through. Later, I received this personal note from JuleAnn as part of the After-Action Review:

"You (Brad) headed out alone up the mountain. We (Jon and Joan Gurley, Lauren Rittman and myself) went into the room at Ridgecrest—I could feel the Holy Spirit on me, and I sensed a boldness to move. The weight was intense. I will admit, I was greatly concerned for you going up on the mountain "alone."

We began praying, and I could see the battle in front of my eyes. I could see swarms of demons attacking from all angles, hissing and raging. There were demons of death, deep dark hatred, rage, murder, etc. It was as if witchcraft was directing them and they were salivating to taste blood and flesh. I know I was praying aloud, but it may have been in tongues. I was aware of Jon, Joan and Lauren, but physically I was feeling pummeled, hit, and beat up. I asked the LORD to bring out the battering ram, as He had spoken to me about the night before, that He would take down this wall the enemy was building to hide and obscure the truth. I continued to declare Jesus as LORD. There were times that the waves of intercession lightened somewhat, and Jon would read intel that corresponded to the Judiciary Committee questioning of Dr. Ford.

Somewhere in that time I also saw into what I would call the enemy's plans for the future. I could see demons in a corral of sorts. There were two corrals, I believe, one for if Brett Kavanaugh was confirmed and one for if he was not confirmed. In other words, the enemy had a plan for either way it went. But I noted the corral pertaining to if he was confirmed. I saw this when I heard myself verbally say *"Brett Kavanaugh will be confirmed."* This corralled mass of demonic energy was like a huge ball or mass of dark putrid evil. Within the blob were hordes of demons that were bloodthirsty and ruthless. They were being held back until their time had come, almost like a rabid dog in a cage. This image alone hurt me to my core, and I had to refocus on Jesus at length. I felt deeply wounded just looking into that blackness. I also noticed after seeing that, I had great fear building up inside me about Brad's safety in being alone on the mountain, the safety of the team, safety for the whole conference, and the safety of our families and country. I needed prayer, so I asked Martha to pray over me. Since that time, I was desperate to debrief with you what I had seen, I guess because it seared into my soul.

After spending some time in the engagement, we as a group felt the burden lift. We all "knew" it was time for us to go to lunch, so we prayed prayers of cleansing and went down to report to Cindy. She informed us that you (Brad) were coming down the mountain and wanted to meet with us. Those things that I saw, I knew you had seen. It was a relief to see you were safe.

I rested during the afternoon of the engagement. I spent most of the time watching the proceedings of Brett Kavanaugh giving his statement and being questioned. I felt as if my heart was going to break, and I found myself interceding for him. I was exhausted.

That night I fell asleep about midnight, only to be awakened by something on my legs. I awoke to searing pain, an intense cramping that twisted my legs. I cried out in pain. Then I could not feel my legs at all, and I was afraid it had severed something. I declared that I belonged to Jesus Christ and commanded this evil presence to leave in Jesus' name. Slowly my legs felt better. I knew it was witchcraft. A cold feeling came over me. I knew I hadn't been alone in that room and believed it had been sent to do something to harm me. I wondered if it was a demon or if witches/satanic worshippers had possibly used astral projection to attack me.

Off-Site Intercessors Also Drawn into the Battle

It is helpful to include one additional perspective from an off-site intercessor in Canada. He was connecting with the engagement through the electronic Discerning the Times newsletter messages I was sending out and through prayer updates from Martin Boardman. He sent the following note sharing that he was strongly called into the battle: (He is a pastor in the Christian Reformed Church and a leader in PRMI ministry. He asked not to be named.)

Hi Brad,
This is __ in Canada. I was gradually drawn into this engagement by the Discerning the Times messages. My initial

response was to pray along the lines suggested in each DTT. I did not join the POTUS cohort for this but prayed a lot about the process. Many of my prayers were for support of the Kavanaughs for protection, strength, and encouragement. I was also praying these things for you. I experienced tiredness and discouragement myself and felt I was picking up on what was being experienced there.

On Thursday, the 27th of September, I watched the hearing all day and was engaged in the Spirit for the whole time. Mostly I was praying in the Spirit, but also for exposure of the deceitful delaying tactics and for truth to shine through. I saw these prayers being answered in a number of ways during the hearing. A particularly striking one was where Dr. Ford was transparent about not being aware of the Senate majority's efforts to deal with her privately and even in California as she requested. The truth that she was maneuvered into the public spectacle by the Democrats for their own reasons became apparent.

The next day, the announcement of the new FBI investigation was a fresh call to prayer for truth to be revealed and for a quick resolution. Also, I was led to pray against any new delaying tactics gaining traction. At some point, I was led to cry out that Brett Kavanaugh was being crucified for the sins of others and asked God to stop this because His Son had already done that work. I am thankful these prayers were answered.

In summary, I would describe my role in the intercession as a supporting one for the discernment team, intercessors, and participants in the hearing. As a Canadian, I believe it was important for us to stand with you in this battle which is not just about your highest court, but also about the attack on our shared Judeo-Christian values.

In Christ and in the battle with you!

(Name withheld by request)

The Conclusion of this Second Engagement

Others on the team reported similar experiences of engagements with high-level demonic powers. But what were the effects of these struggles within the spiritual realm? Did they have any impact on the reality of the process? The immediate impact was that the next day, September 28th, the Judiciary Committee along party lines voted to send Kavanaugh's confirmation to the Senate floor. The decisive factor was when Republican Senator Jeff Flake made his vote contingent upon a one-week FBI investigation into the claims made against Kavanaugh.[70] To me as an intercessor, this felt like a miracle of God's intervention. It was consistent with the word I received from the Lord that Kavanaugh would be confirmed on God's timetable. Frankly, Jeff Flake's call for a one-week delay during which an FBI investigation would be conducted was a very good strategy to enable those senators who still had doubts to more thoroughly consider the issues and have those doubts resolved. After this battle, it felt like the entire nation was on edge waiting for the results of the FBI investigation into the allegations against Kavanaugh. However, in the realm of the Spirit this was a calm before the next storm. The power of the Holy Spirit lifted from me, so I was able to get some sleep and rest up. However, I did not have long to rest and recover before I started to receive guidance again and was called back into the battlespace.

An After-Action Review of this amazing engagement will be covered in the next two chapters.

---

[70]https://www.axios.com/committee-delays-kavanaugh-vote-1538156902-2c78e061-a273-4c47-8ecf-9dcf1b948583.html

Chapter 6 Second Engagement: Phase 2 Clash in the Heavenlies

7

After-Action Review Part A: Second Engagement – Clash in the Heavenlies

I aptly named the prayer battle we just engaged in, "The Clash in the Heavenlies." As I read my report of the engagement, I realized that if I had not experienced it myself, I would have thought this group of intercessors had lost their minds. Their supposed experience raised a host of questions! Were these objectively real and verifiable events? Or were their reports imaginative literary creations filled with metaphors and exaggerations? What did these bizarre experiences dealing with allegedly high-level demonic beings have to do with the Senate Judiciary Committee and the testimonies of Dr. Ford and Judge Kavanaugh?

The After-Action Review's (AAR) greatest challenge is to move past the basic questions about the nature of religious experiences, which many who have been on the frontlines of intercession and spiritual warfare have already resolved through study and personal experience. Many may find it difficult to press through the AAR without having their basic questions and concerns about the engagement addressed.[71] However, I must remain faithful to the objective of discussing the timeless, strategic lessons that guide intercessors and spiritual warriors in prayer battles.

The "Clash in the Heavenlies" presented a rich learning experience for understanding prayer battles. Therefore, we will break this After-Action Review into two chapters. Part A will discuss some basic questions concerning preparation for the engagement that were asked in the After-Action Review by intercessors and those taking part in the event we were called out of.

Questions About Guidance

"How did you and the others get the guidance that you were to leave the meeting room and go to another location for the engagement? And How did you know this was really from the Lord?"

This question leads to the basic issue of how do we distinguish between the voice of God, the leadings of our own thoughts and imaginations, and the voice or influences of evil spirits?

I have assumed throughout this book that God does indeed provide guidance to us, His friends and coworkers. Furthermore, I believe we can distinguish the leading of the Holy Spirit in our

---

[71]To have basic questions about the engagement answered, I suggest participation in PRMI's Dunamis Project equipping process which offers systematic biblical teaching on all the topics touched on in this book. See the PRMI Web page www.prmi.org. See my book, *Passage Through the Wilderness: A Journey of the Soul,* Chosen Books. There I describe in some detail how invisible entities such as angels and demons are experienced. https://www.prmi.org/product/passage-through-the-wilderness/. There are many excellent works and studies on this subject of religious experience. I would highly recommend two great classics: *The Varieties of Religious Experience: A study in Human Nature*, published in 1902. *Mysticism: A Study in Nature and Development of Spiritual Consciousness* by Evelyn Underhill, first published in 1911.

imagination and emotions from those phenomena that are coming from demons. A key concept on how to distinguish the voice of God from other voices is found in Jessie Penn-Lewis's book *War on the Saints*, written out of the experience of the Welsh Revival between 1904-1905.

In a section entitled "How to Detect the Source of a Voice," she writes:

> In order to detect which is the "voice of God," and which is the "voice of the devil," we need to understand that the Holy Spirit alone is charged to communicate the will of God to the believer, and that He works from *within the spirit* of the man enlightening the understanding (Eph. 1: 17-18), so as to bring him into intelligent co-working with the mind of God.
>
> The purpose of the Holy Spirit is, briefly, the entire renewal of the redeemed one, in spirit, soul, and body. He therefore directs all His working to the liberation of every faculty, and never in any way seeks to direct a man as a passive machine, even into *good*. He works in him to enable him to choose the good, and strengthens him to act, but never— even for "good"—dulls him, or renders him incapable of free action, otherwise He would nullify the very purpose of Christ's redemption on Calvary, and the purpose of His own coming.
>
> When believers understand these principles, the "voice of the devil" is recognizable, *i.e.*,
>
> (1) when it comes from outside the man, or within the sphere of his circumference,[72] and not from the central depth of his spirit, where the Holy Spirit abides;
>
> (2) when it is imperative and persistent, urging sudden action without time to reason, or intelligently weigh the issues;
>
> (3) when it is confusing and clamorous, so that the man is

---

[72]I am assuming this term "within the sphere of his circumference" to mean from bodily sensations and emotions in distinction from the inner depth of the person.

hindered from thinking; for the Holy Spirit desires the believer to be intelligent, as a responsible being with a choice, and will not confuse him so as to make him incapable of coming to a decision.[73]

This observation is a good rule for discernment. It is the Holy Spirit who dwells within our spirit, speaks within us without violating our own wills, and allows us the freedom to discern and obey the guidance received, making us coworkers with the Lord. The voice of evil spirits, on the other hand, is from without. Or, if it is still inside of us in our emotions, body or soul, it tends to violate the fundamental principle of our freedom as coworkers and friends of Jesus. While there are certainly times when the Holy Spirit may be very urgent and compelling, as He was in calling us intercessors into this engagement, He always allows us room to discern and decide to walk in obedience. The foundational principle: The Holy Spirt honors our freedom while the Devil violates it, provides a sure guide to sorting out if the "voice" within is from the Lord or from some other source.

Added to this foundational principle, are the Four Discernment Questions or tests that PRMI has developed to be applied to any guidance that is received or any manifestation of the Holy Spirit.[74]

These discernment questions are:

1. DOES IT GIVE GLORY TO JESUS CHRIST IN THE PRESENT AND IN THE FUTURE? –John 14:26, John 16:13-14

2. IS IT CONSISTENT WITH THE INTENTIONS AND CHARACTER OF GOD AS REVEALED IN SCRIPTURE? – John 2:22, 2 Tim.

---

[73]From the profoundly discerning book by Jessie Penn-Lewis, *War on the Saints, in Collaboration with Evan Roberts.* From the experiences of the Welsh Revival, Chapter 6, *War on The Saints.* Home page by Jessie Penn-Lewis, with Evan Roberts, World Wide Web Edition (Based on the Unabridged 1912 Edition) http://www.apostasynow.com/wots/Contents.html

[74]https://www.prmi.org/four-discernment-tests/

3:14-17

3. DO OTHER PEOPLE WHO ARE FILLED WITH THE HOLY SPIRIT HAVE A CONFIRMING WITNESS? — 1 Cor. 14:29

4. IS THERE CONFIRMATION IN OBJECTIVELY VERIFIABLE EVENTS OR FACTS? — Deut. 18:21-22, Isa. 55:10-11

The rigorous application of these four questions among intercessors is an important part of the After-Action Review. It helps them discern whether they are indeed listening to the Holy Spirit or being carried away by their emotions or imaginations. We fully assume the possibility that we can and may be deceived by evil spirits.

In keeping with the rule of discernment that the Holy Spirit respects our freedom of will and involves us in advancing His Kingdom, not as slaves or puppets, but as friends and coworkers, we were given time to be deliberate and rational in preparation for this battle.

Discerning Our Roles in the Upcoming Engagements

The day before the battle, I was aware of the possibility that the Lord might call me and others out of the meeting and up the mountain into an engagement. I shared this possibly with Rev. Cindy Strickler who, as the Director of PRMI and Dunamis Fellowship International, had spiritual authority over the event and the ministry. She had also been an Aaron-type intercessor for me for many years, and had on previous occasions prayed for me as I was called up the mountain to pray. So, she prepared the entire group for this contingency by designating Trever Peyton to take my place as teacher if I should be called out. She also planned for other intercessors to step in to cover the event if some of the intercessors should be called out. In addition, she was in communication with Martin, our Prayer Mobilizer in Canada, to have the off-site intercessors ready and alert.

On the day of the battle, each team member received guidance from the Holy Spirit about being called out of the big meeting. This guidance came in different ways for each person. JuleAnn started to see mental pictures of demons gathering over the US Capital. She also began to feel an intense swirling of emotions and a growing strife, both signs she previously learned were indications the Lord was calling her into a prayer battle. She also experienced the call to stand in the gap alongside me as a co-Moses, a role she had filled before. Martha felt certain she was called to join the team, but as she started to leave the room, felt a deep unease, realizing it would be too dangerous for her to personally join this battle. She felt the Holy Spirit say that from the safety of the gathered community, she was needed to provide prayer cover for the meeting and for the cohort being deployed. Jon did not feel any emotion, but a heightened awareness of the significance of the news reports that were flooding his phone. He logically saw how events about to take place on the Senate floor required special prayer covering, and that events were hurtling toward a political and spiritual confrontation. Joan, Jon's wife, felt a deep sense of love for the cohort team members as well as for Judge Kavanaugh and his family and all they were facing. She wanted to provide love and friendship for those in both the battle on earth and in the spiritual realm.

There were, of course, many more people involved, each with their own story of how the Lord led them into this time of prayer. This account, however, reveals the diversity of the ways the team received guidance. Together and individually we actively discerned our roles, all the while aware that Jesus our Commander, through the Holy Spirit, was positioning His prayer warriors and angelic forces in the multidimensional visible and invisible battlespaces.[75] Satan was, no doubt, also aligning his human and demonic forces for the battle. Some of the intercessors saw this alignment of demonic powers in the spirit. Others inferred this positioning taking place based on the analysis of the news reports coming in.

---

[75]I will explain in more detail the concept of battlespace in the next chapter.

The discernment gathered as a team through the careful collecting and assessment of information coming from both the news media as well as through the revelatory gifts of the Holy Spirit such as prophecy and words of knowledge and the Bible is characteristic of the way the Lord works to provide guidance while honoring us as His coworkers and friends.

Discerning My Call to Leave the Cohort and go Alone Up the Mountain

As I started to teach the large group the morning of the prayer engagement, I received the guidance from the Holy Spirit within me saying that I only had about thirty minutes to do so before He would be shifting the anointing from teaching to prayer. As I progressed through my outline, I was eager to make my third and strongest point. But within me I knew I was no longer teaching in the empowerment of the Holy Spirit, but rather out of my own enthusiasm and egotism to make my third point. I found myself debating with the Lord, "I just need to finish this point." I knew I was perfectly free to not obey, yet knew that I would be stepping out of the flow of what the Holy Spirit was doing if I kept teaching. I was thankful at that moment that the Lord sent some help. Jon came in, waved at me, and pointed to his watch to indicate the beginning of the Kavanaugh hearing. I knew this was a confirmation that the Lord was speaking to me and calling me out. Reluctantly, I handed the microphone to Rev. Peyton. I later learned how the Holy Spirit had fallen upon him for greatly anointed teaching in which he covered the third point of the teaching outline better than I could have.

The process of receiving and discerning this guidance as from the Lord and then acting upon it is an example of how the Holy Spirit continually works in each team member within a prayer cohort. The moment we stop listening and discerning, and instead take for granted that any word heard or strong emotion felt is always from the Lord, that is when we will be deceived.

Questions About Teamwork

"Why was it necessary for Brad to go up the mountain and not join the cohort? Did this not violate PRMI's own teaching on the importance of team work?" These questions were asked by many people during the After-Action Review.

Believe me, I would have loved to have stayed with the rest of the cohort where I knew there was love, fellowship, and protection. I am not sure why I was called out alone, but I have experienced it many times before. It must be for the same reason that Jesus would again and again leave the fellowship of His disciples and go to a lonely place to be with the Father. I had to do the same. Without the distraction of others, I could be in better communion with the Father. I did not feel I was going alone. I was intensely aware of the presence of the Holy Spirit. I also felt undergirded by the large network of prayer intercessors, both on site and around the world, who were providing prayer coverage, as well as by the cohort the Lord had formed. I especially felt the cover, love, connection and support from several Aaron and Hur intercessors, especially Cindy and Jon.

I found out later that the rest of the team had been confused as to why I abandoned them and did not join them in the prayer room. This was my fault. I did not clearly explain the kind of guidance I was receiving. Also, when Jon called to inquire of my whereabouts, I was still trying to sort out what the Lord was calling me to do. I think there was also the human hesitancy to fully commit myself to the leading of the Holy Spirit who I knew was calling me into a major ordeal. Another major factor to consider was the mounting spiritual warfare. Intercessors often experience this scrambling of communication and thoughts. It is all part of Satan's tactics to prevent us from working as a team and to prevent us from moving into the prayer engagement that the Father is calling us into.

Satan vigorously assaulted me with his tactics as I hiked to the designated place up the mountain where the battle was to take place. I experienced irrational bouts of fear, as well as images of bears or big foot stalking me. These attacks were aggravated by the constant mist and rain. I knew the terror and confusion were from the Devil and were intended to force me to turn back to the comfort and safety of the group. I would have done so, except that John Chang was prompted by the Holy Spirit to call me right at my lowest point. Even as Satan's vicious attacks intended to prevent me from going alone to the place of engagement were taking place, they confirmed to me that the Holy Spirit was indeed calling me out alone.

In retrospect, these attacks of fear and confusion seemed obvious and simple to overcome by the blood of the Lamb. But in the moment, they were anything but easy to discern and to overcome.

The Dynamic of Withdrawal and Return

There is a deeper dynamic that can help us understand why the Lord may call the intercessor into a time alone. This is the dynamic of withdrawal and return. The first motion is the Holy Spirit calling the intercessor or spiritual leader to withdraw from the distractions of interacting with others so that he or she can focus on communion and communication with God the Father, Son, and Holy Spirit. This withdrawal is an inward spiritual separating oneself from the material and human realm that is often facilitated by an actual physical withdrawal of oneself to a place to be alone with God. This may take place like it did for Moses going alone up Mount Sinai or for Jesus going to a lonely place to pray. These physical and geographic locations may be transcended to include Jesus' coworker being caught up into the spiritual realm—or into what may be called, "the heavenlies." This took place when Jesus included Peter, James, and John in His withdrawal up the mountain. From that geographic location they were together caught up in the spiritual realm and saw Jesus in resurrection and second person of the Trinity glory having a conversation with Moses and Elijah. (Mathew 1&:1-13)

The events that take place during this time of separation depend upon God's plans and purposes. One may be given revelations, visions for Kingdom work may be conceived, and there may be battles with Satan.

The second movement is to return from this time apart and to rejoin the human community where the implementation of the work done alone with God must continue to take place. It does neither the Kingdom nor the world any good if the intercessor just remains alone on the mountain. After the engagement in the heavenlies was over, Jesus, Peter, James, and John had to go down the mountain and reengage in the world to complete their mission. This movement of return for us is critical for the carrying through of the Father's plans and intentions that were revealed or launched while alone on the mountain.

This dynamic of withdrawal and return and the profound consequences for human history and the kingdom are illustrated in both Moses and Jesus, as well as a host of other great intercessors and spiritual leaders. For instance, Moses went alone up Mount Sinai, the mountain of God, where he had an extraordinary encounter with God and received the Ten Commandments. He then returned down the mountain to present what God had given to the Hebrews who had been liberated from slavery and thus launched the Jewish people as a "kingdom of priests and a holy nation" through whom God would bless all humanity. (Exodus 19:4-7)

Jesus practiced the dynamic of withdrawal and return repeatedly through His earthly ministry. He regularly withdrew alone into the wilderness for deep communion with the Father. For instance, on one occasion he withdrew up the mountain and spent all night in prayer. He returned and called the twelve whom He named Apostles to follow Him. (Luke 6:12-16) On at least two occasions He battled with Satan—once in the wilderness and the other time in the Garden of Gethsemane. On the first of these occasions Jesus returned in great empowerment of the Holy Spirit to heal, to cast out demons, and to preach. (Luke 4) In the second occasion after surrendering to the Father's will in the garden, Jesus returned to go through the agony of the crucifixion. Jesus' ultimate time of withdrawal was on the Cross. We now await His return in glory and the restoration of all things in the New Heaven and New Earth. On two occasions withdrawing by Himself, He took a few disciples with Him and gave them a glimpse of what took place during these alone times. Once was during the transfiguration when Jesus and His disciples were caught up in a vision with Moses and Elijah. The other occasion was when they accompanied Jesus part way into the agony of the Garden of Gethsemane. In each of these examples the times of withdrawal were the occasions when the battle was fought and won, and the return resulted in advancement of the Father's Kingdom purposes.

A modern example of the dynamic of withdrawal and return is seen in the life of Rees Howells, a prayer intercessor during WW II. His biographer Norman Grubb reported that there were days and nights during the battle of Dunkirk when Rees Howells battled alone in prayer. During a time of panic, fearing the Germans would crush the Allied army gathering at Dunkirk and invade England, Rees Howells was called out alone to pray:

"From the night of May 22 to 25 Mr. Howells no longer came to the meetings; other members of the staff took them. He went away alone with God to battle through, and, as others have testified, the crushing burden of those days broke his body. He literally laid down his life..."[76]

My mentor in high-level intercession and spiritual warfare, Archer Torrey, modeled what it meant to go up the mountain alone to engage in prayer battle. I observed him returning from these times, battered, but filled with the joy of the Lord. On a few occasions he invited me to go with him up the mountain in an encounter with high-level demons. Let me share one such incident that I already related in my book, *Discerning the Times: Exposing Satan's plans in Radical Islam.* (Page 110)

The incident happened while I was at Jesus Abbey in South Korea. Archer Torrey, a greatly empowered intercessor, directed the prayer community located in the rugged mountains of the Korean East Coast. One evening, a group of Koreans who lived at

---

[76]Grub, Norman. *Rees Howells Intercessor,* p. 115.

the Abbey and fifteen pastors from Taiwan were called into an engagement with the high-level demons of North Korea. There had been an incident at the DMZ where North Koreans were threatening to attack South Korea. Archer was leading the prayer in Korean, and then in English, which I translated into Chinese. We were praying that the powers of evil would be contained and not able to escalate the tensions to lead into war.

There came a time when the Holy Spirit brought us all into the presence of Jesus Christ with singing in the Spirit, followed by a deep silence full of the glory of God. Then in our own languages, in the name of Jesus Christ, we commanded the powers of evil that were seeking to stir up war to retreat. The prayer time ended, and we concluded with praise. Everyone went off to bed, but I lingered with Archer to debrief the evening. Suddenly we knew that we were not alone. There was a malevolent force pressing in from outside the prayer chapel. Archer smiled! He turned to me and said, "It looks like the Holy Spirit has used our prayers to stir up the Devil and now he is attacking back." Then he shouted, "Hallelujah! The Lord is telling us to step outside and do battle!"

Frankly, I thought Archer had lost his mind! As I hesitated, he bounded up to the altar, snatched up the large wooden cross, and rushed out the door into the bitter cold bright moonlit night. He said, "Come on out!" As I followed him, I stepped into a different dimension of reality. Archer pointed down the mountain valley, saying, "There! Do you see it?" And yes, to my amazement I could see it—a black shape extinguishing all light. At one moment, it seemed to tower over us and take up the whole valley, the next it seemed to be just a point from which emanated intense, life-engulfing evil. Around this presence, like the eye of a tornado, swirled demonic spirits. I knew I was in the presence of a being with the will to destroy the prayer community and all the churches in Korea.

I should have been paralyzed by terror. Instead, I was surprised and heartened to find within myself a steadfastness and a burst of joy at the battle. I started to pray in tongues at the top of my voice. Archer, holding high the cross, speaking with words filled with

Christ's supernatural authority, in Korean, English and in unknown tongues commanded the demon to come no further. There was a moment of struggle; like a blast of a hostile wind that nearly knocked us both down, and then, suddenly like snapping awake after a nightmare, it was gone. Archer put down the cross, lifted his hands shouting praise to Jesus Christ for defeating the powers and principalities by his death on the cross. Archer was so full of joy; it was as if he were a little giddy or even drunk. I was too stunned to say or do anything. As we walked back inside, Archer's comment was, "I just love it when Jesus lets us go with him into battle!" All I could do was to stammer, "What the hell was that?" Archer replied, "You got that right! It was right from hell! No doubt an archon. It may have been Gog, the high-level demon of tyranny; he must have left his headquarters in North Korea and came down here to try to shut down our prayers, but Jesus defeated him."[77]

This incident was a very short dynamic of withdrawal and return, but it made a profound impression on me. It appeared to have made an impact in the spiritual realm, but also with the military situation. After this engagement in the heavenlies, the news reported a decrease in tension and a backing away from the brink of war.

It is important to note that while Archer headed out alone, out the door into the bitter cold moonlit night, a portal into the spiritual realm alone, he called me to join him. We were however not alone, we were also surrounded by an entire community of prayer gathered at Jesus Abbey. The same was true of Rees Howells. He was alone with God battling it out in the heavenlies, but was surrounded and upheld by the prayer community of the Bible College of Wales faculty, staff, and students.

In the prayer battle for Kavanaugh's confirmation, I hiked up the

---

[77]This is a composite of several experiences with high level demons that I had while being mentored by Archer Torrey. On another occasion, after a time of praying for the advancement of the Gospel of Jesus Christ, another archon manifested. Its name was given as Dagon. That was another major prayer battle that took most of the night.

mountain alone to enter a spiritual assignment. But I was not alone at all! I was still part of the cohort who had been called out of the meeting. I was connected and covered by intercessors in the meeting, the cohort and those in the extended network off site. There was also a strong awareness of the love, friendship, prayer and support of the Aaron and Hur intercessors upholding me.

In the one moment when Satan was trying to deceive me into thinking I was alone by overwhelming me with the terror of bears, big foot, and of having a heart attack, the Lord prompted John Chang in New York to call me.

Some reading this book may well be called out alone into these types of engagements. I am sharing the knowledge and experience of the clash in the heavenlies so you will not think you are going crazy when this beckoning from the Holy Spirit starts to happen. However, it is imperative that you are a part of a larger prayer community to help you discern whether or not you are being called out alone. Secondly, it is critically important that you ensure you are surrounded by strong prayer support of both Aaron and Hur type intercessors who will uphold you when you are called into this dynamic of withdrawal and return.

Questions About Preparation

"What preparation was done by Brad and the team before entering the prayer battle?"

There was a long period of preparation as I hiked up the mountain. I was asking the Lord to fill me with the Holy Spirit and give me the power and authority needed to cooperate with Him in the battle ahead. I read some scripture on my phone and lingered on Colossians 1:15-20 about the supremacy of Christ over all things.

I was preparing myself for battle by joyfully summitting myself to Jesus Christ, committing myself to follow Him no matter what was ahead or what the cost, even if it meant being taken out. That may sound a little extreme, but I have dealt with high-level demons before and experienced firsthand their rage and hatred of God turned against the followers of Jesus. The vision of war in heaven described in the book of Revelation fails to prevent the incarnation and mission of Jesus Christ: "So the dragon became enraged at the woman and went away to make war on the rest of her children, those who keep God's commandments and hold to the testimony about Jesus."(Revelation 12:17) That is just what they do; enraged, they make war against us, and it can be vicious, destructive, and even physically fatal.

As I got myself ready for the battle, I surrendered myself to the Lord and entrusted my life, my physical being, my family, the ministry—everything, into His hands. This is a way of dying to oneself!

All the preparation of the team for spiritual battle was a process of stepping into a place of authority for intercession and warfare. It involved letting the Holy Spirit take us to the place Paul speaks of in Ephesians 2:6 "...he raised us up with him and seated us with him in the heavenly realms in Christ Jesus...." This is difficult to describe, but as I continued my walk up the mountain, I knew that it was taking place. By the time I arrived at the lookout place, I was fully surrendered and ready for the assignment ahead—I was sitting with Jesus Christ in the heavenly realms.

The rest of the cohort who had been called to the prayer room had also gone through a similar process of preparation. This consisted of corporate confession and clothing themselves with the armor of God.

In the next chapter we continue this after-action review of the clash in the heavenlies in which I introduce the concept of the three battlespaces and the spiritual weapons that we were led to deploy within those battlespaces.

8

After-Action Review Part B: The Second Engagement— The Weapons of our Warfare

Let us continue this After-Action Review of the battle that took place on September 27th when both Dr. Ford and Judge Kavanaugh presented their testimonies. During this time, the Holy Spirit called out from the general network of intercessors gathered at the Dunamis event and online, a small cohort of intercessors who engaged in a battle in the heavenlies with high-level demonic beings.

The prayer battle to confirm Brett Kavanaugh to the Supreme Court took place in different phases and battlespaces. Before we can fully grasp the nature of the battle and track the different movements of the intercessors, we must have a rudimentary understanding of the three different battlespaces.

Introducing the Concept of the Three Battlespaces

The concept of different battlespaces is derived from the nature of a demonic stronghold. A stronghold is a human and demonic organization with an interface between the hierarchy of demonic beings and an organized hierarchy of humans within a social organization. Centralized human structures like the Nazi party or ISIS correspond to the demonic hierarchy. Hell is a totalitarian dictatorship, so it is not surprising that Satan duplicates totalitarian structures on earth where the highest-level demonic beings possess and work through people at the highest level of the human hierarchy who wield great authority and power. From the top down, myriads of demons interface with every level of the human organization.

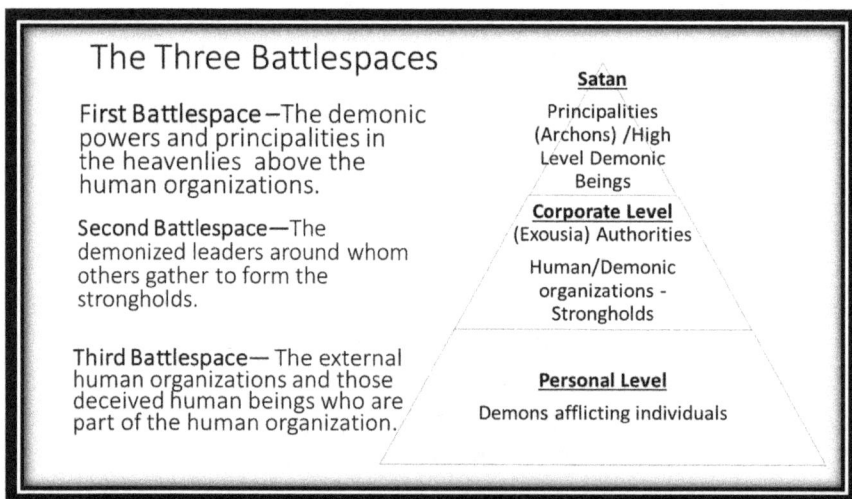

The Three Battlespaces

First Battlespace –The demonic powers and principalities in the heavenlies above the human organizations.

Second Battlespace—The demonized leaders around whom others gather to form the strongholds.

Third Battlespace— The external human organizations and those deceived human beings who are part of the human organization.

Satan

Principalities (Archons) /High Level Demonic Beings

Corporate Level (Exousia) Authorities

Human/Demonic organizations - Strongholds

Personal Level Demons afflicting individuals

In identifying the three battlespaces, we are not inferring the order of the battle, but only the different contexts that we may be called to engage. Cooperating with the Holy Spirit in each battlespace often requires different specific tactics and strategies of intercession and spiritual warfare.

1. The First Battlespace—Engaging the Demonic Powers

The first battlespace is the engagement with the demons in the highest level of their hierarchy in the spiritual realm. These demons are behind humans and their human structures. This first battlespace is identified by St. Paul in Ephesians 6:12:

"For our struggle is not against flesh and blood, but against the rulers, against the powers, against the world rulers of this darkness, against the spiritual forces of evil in the heavens."

Our calling is to be in cooperation with the Holy Spirit and in the authority of Jesus Christ to break the power of the demons and ultimately to divide the kingdom of Satan.

2. The Second Battlespace—the Demonized Leaders of the Stronghold

The second battlespace is the interface between demons and the cadre of human leaders around whom the political or social organization has formed that constitutes the stronghold. This human and demonic interface is made possible because of strongholds in the minds and the hearts of leaders where there is a rejection of God's rule and an adherence to the lies of Satan that oppose God and His Kingdom. These heart and mind strongholds are identified by Paul in 2 Corinthians 10:4-5. "... for the weapons of our warfare are not human weapons, but are made powerful by God for tearing down strongholds. We tear down arguments and every arrogant obstacle that is raised up against the knowledge of God, and we take every thought captive to make it obey Christ."

These core leaders and the human organization and culture that grow up around them give the demonic powers access to influence the minds of all those captivated by the stronghold. Such access takes place because of the ungodly ideologies, hatreds, and demonic attachments that the core leaders carry with them to infect the corporate culture of the entire organization.

In the second battlespace, we are often called to implement strategies and tactics to separate these core leaders from the influence of demonic spirits. We are called to pray that they will be removed from positions of human leadership or so compromised in their ability to lead that Satan will no longer be able to impact social organizations through them.

Most of the prayer battles during the Kavanaugh confirmation hearing took place in this second battlespace as we prayed for the leaders through whom Satan was working to implement his schemes. For instance, we were led to pray for those who were behind the protests and behind the orchestration of charges being brought against Judge Kavanaugh. During the testimony of Dr. Ford, many were led to pray for the liberal activist attorneys sitting behind her who appeared to be her handlers.

On the positive side, intercessors prayed for the protection, empowerment, wisdom, and guidance of the core leaders who embodied Judeo-Christian values. Furthermore, we were led to pray for Judge Kavanaugh and the Republican Senate leaders on the front lines of the battle. (In a future AAR I will be introducing the concept that these people are the "Joshua" workers through whom God's plans are being carried out.)

3. The Third Battlespace—The External Human Organizations and Material Means of the Stronghold

The third battlespace is the outward human organizational aspects of the stronghold. These are the many people who have been enslaved in the system, have imbibed the deceptive ideology, and willingly or unwillingly have become the means through whom Satan is now carrying out his purposes.

In this battlespace, the role of the intercessor will often be to pray for victims to be set free from the stronghold. This involves praying that they be brought to living faith in Jesus Christ, and thus transferred from the empire of Satan to the Kingdom of God. It involves praying to have their minds enlightened with the truth that will correct their deceptive ideologies. Also, in many cases, there is a need for healing of their wounds that have given ground to Satan and made them vulnerable to deception.

In the third battlespace of the Kavanaugh hearings, intercessors were called to pray for the individual protesters. They were especially called to pray for Dr. Christine Ford who seemed so obviously wounded and a victim used by those in power. Perhaps the actual controllers, handlers, or representatives of the human and demonic hierarchy orchestrating this attack were the two attorneys sitting behind her. The true nature of their controlling relationship was exposed when Dr. Ford indicated that they had never communicated to her the multiple attempts the Republican Committee made to take her allegations seriously and to honor her request for privacy. This was such an important revelation of the second and third battlespaces. We were finding verifiable evidence that Dr. Ford was the victim of manipulation by those leaders. This information was provided in the transcript from Judicial Watch: (Rachel Mitchell, the sex crimes prosecutor whom the Republicans on the Judiciary Committee had hired conducted the questioning of both Dr. Ford and Judge Kavanaugh.)

Mitchell's questioning at the hearing continued:

"MITCHELL: Was it communicated to you by your counsel or someone else, that the committee had asked to interview you and that – that they offered to come out to California to do so?

BROMWICH: We're going to object, Mr. Chairman, to any call for privileged conversations between counsel and Dr. Ford. It's a privileged conversation ...

(CROSSTALK)

GRASSLEY: Would – could – could we – could you validate the fact that the offer was made without her saying a word?

FORD: Can I say something to you – do you mind if I say

something to you directly?

GRASSLEY: Yes.

FORD: I just appreciate that you did offer that. I wasn't clear on what the offer was. If you were going to come out to see me, I would have happily hosted you and had you – had been happy to speak with you out there. I just did not – it wasn't clear to me that that was the case."

Id. (emphasis added).

[Commentary from Judicial Watch] Thus, it is clear, by Dr. Ford's own testimony, that her attorneys did not communicate the Committee's multiple offers to take her testimony in California, despite the fact that this was Dr. Ford's preferred option. In fact, Dr. Ford testified that she "wasn't clear on what the offer was" and regarded the possibility of investigators taking her testimony in California as "unrealistic" when in fact it had been specifically offered. Id.

When I watched this exchange on the video, I observed the faces of the attorneys. It looked to me like they were disorientated because Dr. Ford answered the question in spite of their objections. It looked to me like they knew their cover had been exposed.

I was up on the mountain when this was taking place, but one of my prayers had been for the Lord to expose Satan's plans and reveal what was taking place with both Dr. Ford and Judge Kavanaugh. I had been led into this third battlespace of praying for Dr. Ford for healing and release from the demonic stronghold that was using her for Satan's purposes of destroying Judge Kavanaugh. When I watched this exchange, I thought, "That looks rather fishy." It felt like a confirmation of what I had been led to pray. But the objective verification came later when I was able to do more research, read the actual letter that the Judiciary Committee had sent to Dr. Ford's attorneys, and see the careful analysis by Judicial Watch and other legal experts.

In the Actual Prayer Battle, We May be Led into All Three Battlespaces.

Another important principle to be learned from this prayer battle is that different teams of intercessors and individual intercessors may have special callings and anointings to cooperate with the Holy Spirit in the different battlespaces. This is evidenced in the many who were led to pray for the protestors and felt great compassion in praying for Christine Ford. It was touching to hear that even Judge Kavanaugh's young daughter was led to pray for Dr. Ford, her father's accuser, during family prayer time.

Another lesson was learned from this encounter. As the Lord called intercessors from battlespace #3 into battlespace #2, and then into battlespace #1, He activated the "Gideon effect." This is where the Lord reduces the prayer army of many intercessors to a small focused cohort, even to one or two people, who enter into the heavenly battlespace #1. In this battlespace #1, it was JuleAnn and I. The reason for this is that as an intercessor moves to battlespace #1, he or she is called to engage with more and more powerful demonic spirits.

As intercessors move into battlespace #1, the high-level demons are directly engaged. They are no longer mediated through the human organization of demonic strongholds or human agents, but are directly encountered. The battle now shifts from being on earth in the human sphere into the spiritual sphere, or into what Paul called in Ephesians 6:12, the "heavenly places."

Where is the First Battlespace Located?

Where is this sphere where evil spirits have their command and control center and exercise influence over the earth? There is considerable discussion about this. I take guidance from what Paul says in 2 Corinthians 12:2-4.

> I know a man in Christ who fourteen years ago (whether in the body or out of the body I do not know, God knows) was

caught up to the third heaven. And I know that this man (whether in the body or apart from the body I do not know, God knows) was caught up into paradise and heard things too sacred to be put into words, things that a person is not permitted to speak.

What is suggested here is that Paul was caught up into what he called the third heaven and paradise, a different dimension than the created order. This is apparently the location of the throne room of heaven where God dwells, as revealed in Revelation 4 and 5.

I know that in the battle that took place on the mountain top, I was caught up in the heavenlies in the spiritual realm, possibly battling demons on their own turf above the earth and human spheres. I believe I was doing this not from earth looking upward, but from the third heaven sitting with Jesus. (Ephesians 2:6) This would mean it was happening in my own spirit, as I am created in the image of God. When we are born again, we belong to Jesus and sit with Him in the heavenly places.

In our many experiences in spiritual warfare, including when we have been called up into the heavenlies, we have had similar experiences to those described in the Bible. In the case of the Kavanaugh hearings, the battle in the heavenlies was shared with others who were also caught up into the vison. JuleAnn was caught up in the same battle and spiritual sphere that I was in. She experienced it in her own body and soul. I also felt her joining me in the battle as a fellow warrior within the spiritual realm. She was part of the actual vision that was taking place. However, the others in the cohort were not caught up in the vision in the same way she was.

What the others observed were the physical manifestations of the battle taking place in the spiritual realm through JuleAnn's physical body: groaning, struggling, praying in tongues, giving verbal commands, and being physically battered by invisible demons. This was happening within her own spirit which was engaged in the spiritual realm.

Sometimes the battles in the heavenlies/spiritual realms actually break into the human sphere and cause manifestations that may be objectively seen, heard, and felt by other witnesses. I do not think this happened in the present battle, but I am not sure. I have experienced a few battles in which they have.

Steve Aceto and I Experience High-Level Demons

To illustrate this phenomenon of multiple people objectively experiencing spiritual events in the physical realm, I offer this example: It was on the first anniversary of the massacre of students at Columbine High School in Columbine, Colorado, April 20, 1999, which is also the anniversary of the birth of Adolf Hitler. Steve Aceto and I were caught up into the heavenlies for an engagement with high-level evil spirits.[78]

Three days before this anniversary, strange things started to happen in our area. First my daughter called from college having had an experience with a demonic presence. She felt that her little sister Rebecca was in danger at the high school. About the same time, several students were arrested at our high school with a plot to repeat the Littleton attack to commemorate Hitler's birth.

On the evening of the April 19, Steve Aceto (a friend and intercessor) called and suggested that we gather a group to pray for the high school. Fran (Steve's wife and a substitute teacher) had reported that all day the school had been in the grip of fear with a foreboding of impending evil. Security at the high school was pervasive, and there were rumors of a major attack planned for Friday, April 20.

I spent 30 minutes on the phone trying to call other intercessors, but all the phones were tied up. I did send out a prayer alert over email to some of PRMI's intercessors asking for prayer. The only people I was able to reach were Richard and Portia White (our pastor and his wife) but they were tied up with a family event. I

---

[78] I introduced Steve Aceto in footnote 12.

called Steve back. And even though we really wanted others with us, we decided to go pray anyway.

It was about 9:30 when Steve drove down to my house to get me. From the moment he arrived the Holy Spirit fell powerfully upon us. While hardly speaking a word to each other in English, we were caught in the rushing river of the Spirit and simply prayed in tongues.

We were led to pray, "Lord what is going on? Why is this happening?" We drove up to Montreat, then got out by Lake Susan and walked up the steep Graybeard Road. On one side was the stream, on the other vacant summer houses. As we prayed, we sensed that we were coming against some stronghold of fear and of death and that all of this was connected to Nazism. We were also aware that the void in our schools and culture created by those who are stripping Christianity away from our public life had no defenses against this type of evil.

As we got to the top of the last street light, which would have had us at an elevation higher than the high school and well beyond the last house in a mountain wilderness, we felt the Holy Spirit say, "Now stop praying in tongues, and in the authority of the name of Jesus, command that these strongholds be broken." We were aware of great authority and power as we commanded the demonic strongholds to be broken. We then were led to exalt Jesus Christ and to declare His victory over the darkness. Our prayer became "Lord, push back the darkness in our school, our culture and in the hearts of the students." We shifted back into praying in tongues, but this time they were not battle prayers, but the Holy Spirit rejoicing in the wonder and power of Jesus Christ.

We walked as we prayed and were about halfway down when I started to hear a strange babbling noise like distant voices. This was NOT the wind. There was no wind. The summer homes were dark and empty. The dense forest silent. It was too early and cold for night insect sounds. The stream running besides the road was making a familiar natural sound. What we heard was ethereal, and seemed to becoming from up the mountain on one side of the road, and then would drift to the other side, then down in the valley, at times from behind us or ahead of us.

We could not pin down exactly where the voices were coming from, and were not even sure that we were hearing them with our physical ears. One thing was certain—we were both having the same spiritual experience. Then we suddenly realized that we had heard this sound before while taking part in exorcisms. This is the phenomenon called the "voice," and happens in exorcisms when the exorcist hears the babble of the torment of hell and the sounds of evil spirits. Usually the voice comes through or in the presence of the demon possessed person, but we were hearing it directly, unmediated.

Here is a description of the phenomenon by Malachi Martin that fits what we struggle to put into words:

> "Slowly they all began to hear sound. It was, at the beginning, like the sound of a crowd or mob – feet pounding faintly, voices shouting, screaming, yelling, jeering, talking, distant whistling and grunting. They could not fix from what direction it came... The noise sounded nearer, just as confused as ever, but now with one overall mood or note: mourning for an ineluctable sorrow. Listening to that sound on the tape recording of the exorcism, and as it grows louder and louder, one begins to get the conviction of listening to the tortured murmurs and helpless protests of a mob in agony... Over and above all the voices but constantly weaving in and out among them, there was the full scream of a woman orchestrating all the other noises and voices around itself as their theme. It came in great rising and falling curves, louder and fainter, still louder and then fainter, regular, upbeat, jarring, resounding with a passion of pain and lost hope."[79]

When we realized what we were hearing, we were astonished and kept asking each other if it was real. While startled, we were

---

[79]*Hostage to the Devil: The Possession and Exorcism of Five Living Americans* by Malachi Martin. Reader's Digest Press (1976) pp. 244 –245.

not afraid. We felt like we were in a bubble of protection provided by Jesus through a team of intercessors led to stand in the gap for us. We did not feel personally attacked, rather we felt that we were overhearing the demonic invasion that was being pushed back by the power of Jesus Christ.

As we walked down the road, nearly to our car the cacophony of voices grew very distinct, and then a crescendo into a long wavering high-pitched terrifying scream of unspeakable agony, and then it stopped abruptly, as if the door to hell had been slammed shut. By this time we were praying loudly in tongues, giving praise to Jesus Christ, and running as fast as we could in the dark back to the car!

We kept praying as we returned home asking the Lord whether there was any possible ground that could have been given at the high school. Then suddenly Steve remembered two facts: First, the high school had been the site of the old TB hospital with a crematorium where they burned the dead bodies. It was still standing in the woods at the edge of the athletic field. So we prayed against any spirits of death that may have been welcomed into that place. Secondly, during World War II, German prisoners of war had been housed at the TB hospital. This could have been the open door to the Nazi spirits. As we prayed against this, we suddenly felt that our work was done and we could stop praying.

The next day everything was peaceful at the high school. Later a group of pastors from the area prayed through the area asking for cleansing.

Both Steve and I were confused as we were hearing and feeling this voice from hell and experiencing the vivid living presence of Jesus Christ overcoming the evil seeking to invade our community and high school. These events were taking place in multiple dimensions.

Now back to our present battle in the heavenlies with high-level demons that had actual impact on my body and emotions. I was actually in the spiritual realm where Jesus was working through me and my Holy Spirit-led actions to defeat Satan's forces. The same happened to JuleAnn and the cohort team. This felt ambiguity was captured well by Paul when he described how he was caught up into the third heaven and said, "whether in the body or apart from the body I do not know, God knows." (2 Corinthians 12:2-4)

Tactics of Spiritual Warfare in Dealing with this Level of Demons

High-level demonic beings in the heavenly realms have vast numbers of demons at their command. These demons are interwoven in human organizations and in the captive hearts of human leaders. They have claimed "ground" in the hearts of many, which gives them access to the human means to carry out their evil intentions. This makes them very powerful and dangerous.

Therefore, the first tactic for engaging this level of demons is not to engage them, but rather to offer ourselves as the means through whom Jesus Christ engages them. This is true at every level of prayer and spiritual warfare. It is not us, but Christ through the Holy Spirit in us, who intercedes and engages in combat. The battle is the Lord's! But as Jesus' friends and coworkers, He has called us to be the means through whom He intercedes and fights.

To engage in a battle in the heavenlies, it is essential to master the practice of Jesus when He said, "I tell you the solemn truth, the Son can do nothing on his own initiative, but only what he sees the Father doing. For whatever the Father does, the Son does likewise." (John 5:19) We must die to ourselves, completely and totally surrender to Jesus, and radically commit to do what He commands us to do. We find out what His commands are and are able to do what He is doing by listening to the Holy Spirit and being grounded in the Bible as the Word of God. This may sound like a contradiction between God honoring our freedom and the requirement for total surrender. I do not know how to resolve that contradiction except to say that at any point in this battle I knew I had the freedom to turn away from the engagement.

The way the Holy Spirit guides intercessors in high level prayer engagements is comparable to the step by step way He led Philip in Acts 8. First, Philip was led by an angelic visitation to leave the ministry in Samaria and go to the desert road. The Holy Spirit then told Philip, "Go over and join this chariot." The Spirit directed Philip to the exact context where he could cooperate with the Lord in bringing salvation to an Ethiopian eunuch. Having completed that assignment, "the Spirit of the Lord suddenly took Philip away" and later he appeared in another city, Azotus where he continued "preaching the gospel." The Holy Spirit will direct us in the same way; He will guide us to cooperate with Him in engaging with Jesus in defeating demons and accomplishing God's plans.

The Pronouncement to Evil Powers that God Had Chosen Judge Kavanaugh

In this battle, there were many weapons the Lord called me to deploy: praying in tongues, binding demons, cutting demons off from Satan's agents, praying the truth would be revealed and lies exposed, praying for protection of Brett Kavanaugh, moving into praise, and so forth. There was one action, however, that I was led to undertake, that in retrospect, seemed to have been the decisive turning point in the battle.

At one point in the height of the struggle with the high-level spirits, the Lord called me to make a prophetic announcement. I was to proclaim to the demonic powers that God had chosen Judge Brett Kavanaugh to be in this position as a Supreme Court Justice to uphold the Judeo-Christian values upon which America was founded.

Here is what happened as recorded in chapter 6:

> There came a time when the Holy Spirit spoke with perfect clarity that God the Father had chosen Brett Kavanaugh to be in this position on the Supreme Court and in the role to defend the US Constitution against those who would seek to destroy the Judeo-Christian values embodied in the Constitution. Then the Holy Spirit told me that I was to proclaim this fact to

the powers and principalities that were opposing God's will.

I shouted this word out over the mountain valley. As I did, I felt in my spirit and saw in my mind's eye like expanding ripples on a lake, actions being set in motion, resulting in spiritual and human opposition being thrust back and Judge Kavanaugh being installed on the bench of the Supreme Court. It was like Satan's lines of defense were being breached and held open just long enough for the decisions to be made by the human actors for Judge Kavanaugh to be confirmed by the Judiciary Committee.

The Father has chosen to work in the world through people who speak His word. The Holy Spirit uses these faithful believers to accomplish the Father's purposes. There are several Bible passages that help explain the dynamic of God's Word spoken by human beings that is empowered by the Holy Spirit. Here is one:

> "For as the heavens are higher than earth, so are My ways higher than your ways, and My thoughts than your thoughts. (10) For as the rain and snow come down from heaven, and do not return there without having watered the earth, making it bring forth and sprout, giving seed to sow and bread to eat, (11) so My word will be that goes out from My mouth. It will not return to Me in vain, but will accomplish what I intend, and will succeed in what I sent it for." (Isaiah 55:9-11 TLV)

Implied in this passage is the Word going out from "My mouth" is being actually spoken and written by the prophet Isaiah. But God speaking through the anointed person is confirmed in Paul's explanation about the critical role of preaching the Word in the following passage:

> How are they to call on one they have not believed in? And how are they to believe in one they have not heard of? And how are they to hear without someone preaching to them?

(15) And how are they to preach unless they are sent? As it is written, "How timely is the arrival of those who proclaim the good news." (Romans 10:14-15)

Here we see the crucial, spirit-filled dynamic of people speaking truth at the inspiration and guidance of the Holy Spirit.   The Spirit then empowers the word to accomplish its purpose. We see this modeled for us in Jesus.   With the Holy Spirit upon Him in power, He preached the Kingdom of God by calling people to repent and believe. He also spoke words of healing and forgiveness. To the woman about to be stoned to death for committing adultery, he said, "I do not condemn you either. Go, and from now on do not sin anymore." (John 8:11) To the Roman centurion with the sick servant Jesus said, "Go; just as you believed, it will be done for you." The servant was healed. Jesus also spoke to the demons and commanded them out of people: "When it was evening, many demon-possessed people were brought to him. He drove out the spirits with a word and healed all who were sick." (Mathew 8:16)

When God the Holy Spirit gives us a word to speak into a situation where He is desiring to bring change, and that word is met with faith, then the stage is set for dynamic change. For as we speak that word in obedience into the situation at the moment indicated by God, the Spirit empowers the word to create the new reality. This is not a matter of our finding an appropriate scripture to apply to a situation, but of our receiving the guidance from God and acting or speaking it in His timing.

As demonstrated in Jesus' ministry, the dynamic involves people being guided by the Holy Spirit to speak a word in faith consistent with the will of God the Father. The Holy Spirit then uses the word to accomplish its intended purpose.

This dynamic applies not just to Jesus, but to those who are called as His disciples to whom He promised that they would do the same works that He did. (John 14:12) For example, in Acts chapter 3, Peter and John meet the lame man at the Beautiful Gate of the Temple. They were filled with the Holy Spirit and Peter was led to say to the man lame from birth, "I have no silver or gold, but what

I do have I give you. In the name of Jesus Christ the Nazarene, stand up and walk!" This word spoken into the dynamic of the moving of the Holy Spirit had results. "He jumped up, stood and began walking around, and he entered the temple courts with them, walking and leaping and praising God." (Acts 3:8)

Jesus has granted us a similar authority to speak His words into the spiritual realm over evil spirits in which the same word and Spirit dynamic takes place.

> Then the seventy-two returned with joy, saying, "Lord, even the demons submit to us in your name!" (18) So he said to them, "I saw Satan fall like lightning from heaven. (19) Look, I have given you authority to tread on snakes and scorpions and on the full force of the enemy, and nothing will hurt you. (20) Nevertheless, do not rejoice that the spirits submit to you, but rejoice that your names stand written in heaven." (Luke 10:17-20)

I know that Jesus tells us to rejoice that our names are written in heaven instead of in the fact that demons are subject to us in Jesus' name. However, that does not diminish the fact that Jesus gives us spiritual authority over demons and the "full force of the enemy." We have authority to do the works that Jesus did if we believe in Him and act in obedience to the guidance of the Holy Spirit. (John 14:12-14) In the case of the Kavanaugh hearing, it was speaking the Word of God in faith into the heavenly realms, both binding high-level evil spirits as well as announcing that God the Father had chosen Brett Kavanaugh to be in this position on the Supreme Court. This "word" was then used by the Holy Spirit to accomplish God's intentions. The fact that JuleAnn received the same word confirmed that this was not my imagination, but a word from the Holy Spirit. She, however, spoke it out to the members of the cohort who joined in praying that it could come to pass. I, on the other hand, battled with high-level demons in the heavenlies, and was called to declare this to the powers and principalities.

These words were used by God to have impact in the spiritual and earthly spheres because they were spoken according to the well-established principles given in the Bible for how we are to cooperate with Jesus Christ as His friends and coworkers.[80]

I believe the effect of this clash with high-level demons had a profound influence on what happened in the earthly realm. The Judiciary Committee voted along party lines to recommend that Kavanaugh's nomination for confirmation go to the Senate, and that the vote by the full Senate be deferred one week so that a supplemental FBI background check dealing with the allegations could be conducted.

We must move to the next engagement!

---

[80]These principles must be mastered by the intercessors! I do not have the space to teach you these in this book, so I suggest you go to PRMI's web site where we provide extensive equipping on these basic and advanced topics. Go to www.prmi.org

9

Third Engagement: Dividing Satan's Kingdom Phase 1— The Preparation

After the intense political and spiritual struggle to get Judge Kavanaugh through the Judiciary Committee, we entered a lull in the battle. For the intercessors, this was a welcome reprieve from the spiritual engagement. One can sustain the intensity of the Holy Spirit working through us and clashes with demonic beings for only limited periods of time before it starts to take an irreparable toll on our physical and emotional beings. This blessed relief was, I am sure, part of God's provision for us, His human coworkers and friends. God never grows weary, nor do the angels, but we do.

This reprieve is also part of the nature of all engagements involving humans, whether in the spiritual realm or on earthly battlefields. The following distinct but fluid phases take place:

- A season of preparation of the army
- Getting positioned in the battlespace

- The clash with the enemy
- Leading to either victory, defeat or stalemate
- Rest and recovery, which is preparation for the next engagement

These phases were well illustrated in the second engagement. We then moved out of the battle into a time of rest and recovery, and did what we always do as a team—conduct an after-action review of what happened. As most of us returned home, the AAR took place over the internet and through phone calls. We were then called back into what was to be the third engagement.

The Events in the Human Realm

Before we explain the prayer work in the spiritual dimension, a brief review of the events during the week before the full Senate vote was taken on October 6, 2018 will provide the context.

It seemed like the whole nation entered a time of suspenseful waiting. The compromise arrived at by the Committee members and the White House was for a one-week extension before the vote by the Senate for the FBI to do the supplementary background checks on Judge Brett Kavanaugh. The intention was to check any evidence corroborating the charges of sexual misdeeds that had been so stridently brought against him. It seemed that the protesters took a breather. They were still present, but either not as disruptive or the press was not giving them much attention.

The Guidance of How to Pray

Over the weekend, I sent an e-mail notice to a select team of intercessors who had signed up for the POTUS Prayer Network. This team consisted of around fifty people who had received a specific call to pray for President Trump and the fulfillment of God's agenda through him and the administration. This diverse group were from Canada, the UK, and the USA, and were of different political perspectives and party affiliations. They were not involved to play politics, but to pray and to take part in advancing the Kingdom of Yeshua/Jesus.

This was my notice:

First, we must continue to pray for piercing Satan's cloaking that is hiding both the schemes of Satan and those of human beings whose plans and actions are consistent with the plans to prevent originalist judges being placed onto the Supreme Court.

We are to pray that these lies and schemes will be exposed for all to see so that they may be countered.

We must pray that if Judge Kavanaugh is guilty of these allegations, that he will be exposed; and if he is not guilty, that he will be vindicated.

Second, we must pray for the protection of God's plans through President Trump and the selection of judges to the Supreme Court.

Let me state my opinion here: I am convinced that Brett Kavanaugh IS one of those judges whose impeccable judicial record as well as character confirm that he is an originalist and well suited to serve on the Court.[81]

Let me take a risk here: While on the mountain in prayer, I heard the Lord saying that Brett Kavanaugh was the person He had chosen to fill that seat. [JuleAnn received the same guidance—however, I did not know that at the time I sent out this note.] I was called by the Holy Spirit to announce that this was God's intention in the heavenly realms in the authority and the name of Jesus Christ. As I had made this proclamation—I shouted out into the mist-shrouded gorge, first in tongues and then as a prophetic word in English and Chinese. As I did, I had been given a glimpse in the spiritual

---

[81]https://www.facebook.com/officialbenshapiro/posts/ashley-kavanaugh-asked-that-christians-pray-psalm-40-over-their-family-powerful-/2182794215091329/

realm of the word spoken being connected with the working of the Holy Spirit and moving toward its fulfillment. I also could see the forces of hell in vivid images, as well as those of the Radical Left aligned together and fighting against God's intentions being fulfilled within human affairs.

I had also received the guidance that God's Kingdom plans would not prevail over Satan's schemes without our being faithful to the work of prayer according to the Holy Spirit's guidance. We must be ready to discern and to instantly obey any commands the Lord should give us.

We are to pray for God's intervention constraining the powers of death, destruction, anarchy, and deception. But we must also pray for those through whom He will bring His intervention. Further, we are to pray for wise decisions and actions on the part of Congress and the White House.

Third, we are to pray according to Ashley Kavanaugh's appeal that we pray Psalm 40:13-14.

The best guidance as to how to pray for the rest of the week was given by Ashley Kavanaugh who sent out the following notice on September 29th:

Ashley Kavanaugh asked that Christians pray Psalm 40 over their family. Powerful Psalm. Verses 13-14: "Be pleased O Lord to deliver me, make haste to help me. Let them be ashamed and confounded together that seek after my soul to destroy it; let them be driven backward and put to shame that wish me evil." #Iwillprayinsupportof Kavanaugh (Amy Dixon to Ben Shapiro September 29.)[82]

So please pray for Brett and Ashley Kavanaugh and their family. Also pray for those senators from both parties to not be deceived; and for those who are deceived, to be unable to conspire together to take part in Satan's schemes to destroy

---

[82]https://www.facebook.com/officialbenshapiro/posts/ashley-kavanaugh-asked-that-christians-pray-psalm-40-over-their-family-powerful-/2182794215091329/

America.

Fourth: Pray for the love of God to flood the floor of the Senate.

Missy in South Carolina received the following guidance on July 1, 2018, which is relevant for this week leading up to the vote. (She was out in the fields picking blackberries when the Holy Spirit surprised her by falling on her and started speaking to her through words and visions.) She wrote:

"He kept telling me to pray for His love to flood the floor of the Senate so that as folks left, they would know that they had been in the presence of God Almighty. It was similar to the scene where after Elijah's showdown with the prophets of Baal, the people's response was, 'The Lord, he is God.' I felt led to pray that the world would see this and know that there is a God."

"Next, my prayer began to focus on those in the Senate who loved Jesus but had been deluded by false ideology— that God open their eyes and that they would stand up for Jesus on the floor of the Senate."

With that guidance, we entered this week of waiting.

God Begins to Answer these Prayers

The week started uneventfully; there were no big clashes, just a pressing in along the lines above. For me I prayed into Psalm 40, especially verses 13-14: "Be pleased O Lord to deliver me, make haste to help me. Let them be ashamed and confounded together that seek after my soul to destroy it; let them be driven backward and put to shame that wish me evil."

As we were praying, we started to observe some hopeful signs that God was answering our prayers. Reports started to filter out vindicating Judge Kavanaugh. From what I saw, none of these reports seemed to get as much attention in the national media as the allegations of sexual misconduct had. But they did reverberate through the more conservative media through Bill O'Reilly, Ben

Shapiro, Shawn Hannity, and Rush Limbaugh. But these were ignored voices crying in the wilderness. Our role as intercessors was to discern whether these reports were true, and if they were, to pray that they would be used by the Lord to answer the prayer of Psalm 40:13-14.

The Report from Rachel Mitchell

The first answered prayer and vindication of Kavanaugh was a report from Rachel Mitchell. She was hired by the Republicans to question both parties in a fair and balanced way. In the glare of national media coverage, she had methodically questioned both Dr. Ford and Judge Kavanaugh before the Judiciary Committee. The questions were direct, some embarrassingly personal, but all asked in a deeply respectful way to Dr. Ford and Judge Kavanaugh, and the Senators at the hearing.[83]

Rachel Mitchell's integrity is confirmed in a memorandum sent to all Republican senators:

Memorandum[84]

TO: All Republican Senators
FROM: Rachel Mitchell, Nominations Investigative Counsel
United States Senate Committee on the Judiciary
DATE: September 30, 2018
RE: Analysis of Dr. Christine Blasey Ford's Allegations:

This memorandum contains my own independent assessment of Dr. Ford's allegations, based upon my independent review of

---

[83]To get a feel for the way she asked the questions and the answers that she received I suggest you view the hearing. You will need to watch the whole process as I have not been able to find any video just of her questions and their answers. https://www.c-span.org/event/?451895/judge-kavanaugh-professor-blasey-ford-testify-sexual-assault-allegations

[84]https://assets.documentcloud.org/documents/4952137/Rachel-Mitchell-s-analysis.pdf

the evidence and my nearly 25 years of experience as a career prosecutor of sex-related and other crimes in Arizona. This memorandum does not necessarily reflect the views of the Chairman, any committee member, or any other senator. No senator reviewed or approved this memorandum before its release, and I was not pressured in any way to write this memorandum or to write any words in this memorandum with which I do not fully agree. The words written in this memorandum are mine, and I fully stand by all of them. While I am a registered Republican, I am not a political or partisan person.[85]

In the Executive Summary of her report, her conclusion is as follows:

In the legal context, here is my bottom line: A "he said, she said" case is incredibly difficult to prove. But this case is even weaker than that. Dr. Ford identified other witnesses to the event, and those witnesses either refuted her allegations or failed to corroborate them. For the reasons discussed below, I do not think that a reasonable prosecutor would bring this case based on the evidence before the Committee. Nor do I believe that this evidence is sufficient to satisfy the preponderance-of-the-evidence standard.[86]

This memorandum contained the careful point by point review

---

[85]Pg. #1 of the Memorandum:
https://assets.documentcloud.org/documents/4952137/Rachel-Mitchell-s-analysis.pdf
[86]Ibid.

of the evidence supporting this conclusion.[87]

CNN reported Rachel Mitchell's conclusions in the headline, *"Outside counsel tells Republican senators 'reasonable prosecutor' would not bring Ford case against Kavanaugh."*[88]

Others, however, doubted if she had enough information to come to the conclusions she came to. These views were reflected in the opinion piece by EJ Montini in the Arizona Republic, *"Rachel Mitchell went from respected prosecutor to political hack: Why would she produce a memo discounting Dr. Christine Blasey Ford's case without an adequate investigation?"*[89]

I found the memo very fair, nonpolitical, persuasive, and validated by the facts. I found the objections to her report to be consistent with the Democratic strategy of seeking to delay the vote for as long as possible by every means possible. In this case, they asked for further investigation. This need was, to some degree valid, and was in fact taking place through the supplemental FBI background checks.

A case of "False Memory Syndrome?"

Some intercessors had raised the question of how could Dr. Ford be so sincere and convinced Brett Kavanaugh had assaulted her decades ago and not be telling the truth.

Frankly, as I watched Dr. Ford's full testimony before the Judiciary Committee, and as she sincerely answered Rachel

---

[87]The following is the opinion piece from Dailywire:
https://www.dailywire.com/news/36519/prosecutor-questioned-ford-shreds-her-case-5-page-ryan-saavedra

[88]https://www.cnn.com/2018/09/30/politics/rachel-mitchell-kavanaugh-ford/index.html

[89]https://www.azcentral.com/story/opinion/op-ed/ej-montini/2018/10/01/rachel-mitchell-christine-blasey-ford-brett-kavanaugh/1491739002/

Mitchell's questions, I had the same question. But apart from the fact that there were many odd discrepancies as well as the lack of corroborating witnesses, all exposed by Mitchell's memo, I was troubled with the possibility that this could be a case of "false memory syndrome."

Memories can be falsified to provide a plausible hypothesis to account for an experience of genuine wounding and suffering. This is a very real possibility in inner healing ministry, counseling, and therapy when a person with deep emotional wounds unconsciously distorts their memory of an event to fit a proposed feasible cause. This cause could be proposed by the counselor or by the milieu in which the wounded person lives.

To provide a firsthand example of this, a few years ago there was considerable emphasis on cases of Satanic ritual abuse. I did in fact conduct healing prayer, deliverance, and exorcism for serval people whose emotional wounding and demonization was caused by having been subjected to terrible satanic rituals. I was able to substantiate the validity of their memories of the satanic abuse by other witnesses who had been subjected to the same rituals by the same coven. However, as Satanic ritual abuse became widely known as a possible source of emotional wounding and demonization, I started receiving many referrals of people who had recently started to remember having been subjected to Satanic rituals decades ago. While the emotional wounding and the affliction by demons proved to be very real, under careful scrutiny we found the cause not to be Satanic ritual abuse, but some more common cause of abuse or neglect by their family members.

The hurt-filled memories, especially when decades old, are especially subject to falsification to fit the wounded person and their therapist's interpretative framework for such hurts. Another common false memory is to attribute sexual abuse to one's father, especially if the father was emotionally absent or unloving. The pain and the emotional wounding are very real, but the "memory" that it was caused by the father's sexual abuse may not be real at all, and may be unverifiable. It could well have been someone other than the father—an uncle or a neighbor. Or perhaps the sexual abuse never happened at all, but was a useful explanation to help explain the very real pain and emotional dysfunction caused by the unloving or absent father.[90]

In the case of Dr. Ford, it seemed clear that she had endured some type of early trauma. The reports all indicate that something like what she described did indeed happen. However, it is very possible that the memory of it being Brett Kavanaugh could have been suggested by Dr. Ford's own political activism as well as those she was associated with.

Given what we know about memory, the fact that a person is sincere and fully convinced that the event happened just as they reported remembering it does not constitute proof that it is true to the facts. All allegations must be verified by corroborating witnesses and verifiable evidence. In the case of Dr. Ford's allegations that Brett Kavanaugh as a high school student assaulted her, her claims were not substantiated by objective evidence, such as a police report, nor by witnesses whom she named as being present at the event.

There seemed to be a well-coordinated campaign underway to prevent even the discussion that Dr. Ford's allegations may not be true to fact. First, and strangely, I started to read articles from left leaning publications asserting that in cases of sexual abuse, a person's memory is an infallible recorder of experience.[91] This seemed intended to discount the possibility that Dr. Ford may be a case of false memory syndrome.

Secondly, obstructing a careful, compassionate, but reasonable

---

[90]The Rev. Cindy Strickler and I wrote about the dynamics of how false memories are formed in our book, *"Let Jesus Heal Your Hidden Wounds: Cooperating with the Holy Spirit in Healing Ministry."*

[91]CHRISTINE FORD, WASHINGTON POST AND JUNK SCIENCE
A leftist propaganda machine pumps out a characteristically atrocious article. October 19, 2018 Christopher DeGroot https://www.frontpagemag.com /fpm/271670/christine-ford-washington-post-and-junk-science-christopher-degroot

review of Dr. Ford's allegations was the movement of "We believe all survivors." "We believe Women." This created an atmosphere where anyone questioning the validity Dr. Ford's allegations was vilified for being opposed to women or of supporting those who abused women.

However, seeping through this smoke screen obscuring the possibility of false memory syndrome was verified evidence that confirmed that Dr. Ford had indeed had a traumatic experience like she described, but not with the accused Brett Kavanaugh. A report was released by the Senate Judiciary Committee on October 5th giving evidence from a witness that Christine Blasey Ford had an encounter similar to what she claimed was by Kavanaugh, but with someone else. This was reported by such conservative media as the Canada Free Press, but was apparently ignored by the liberal media.[92]

I know these reports were coming from conservative news outlets and sources, but the more liberal press and pundits were not as obviously reporting on them nor giving all the facts that were showing up in the Judiciary Committee's reports.

The FBI Completes the Supplementary Background Check

While these were hopeful signs, we all waited for the FBI to complete the supplementary background checks. The much-anticipated report came without much fanfare from the liberal media.

At 3:07 AM On October 4, 2018, Chuck Grassley, the Republican Senator who headed the Judiciary Committee, tweeted:

Supplemental FBI background file for Judge Kavanaugh has been

---

[92]https://canadafreepress.com/article/senate-report-reveals-christine-blasey-ford-had-an-encounter-similar-to-her

received by @senjudiciary Ranking Member Feinstein & I have agreed to alternating EQUAL access for senators to study content from additional background info gathered by non-partisan FBI agents 1/3[93]

Then on October 5, at 10:30am, USA Today reported the results of the FBI report:

"GOP releases summary of FBI report on Kavanaugh: 'No corroboration of the allegations"[94]

I read through all the reports. From the press reactions to the announcement of the FBI reports, it seemed that the liberal press moved into high gear even before they came out to discredit them.[95] However, the preponderance of evidence was growing that Judge Kavanaugh was not only innocent of all the allegations, but was the victim of a vicious, well-funded, masterfully choreographed, smear campaign by the leaders of the Democratic Party in an alliance with the Radical Left.

This was the background for what was to happen in the spiritual realm where intercessors were called back into the heavenlies with the assignment from the Holy Spirit to give the command that Satan's kingdom be divided. It is to this extreme and most dangerous phase of the engagement that we must now turn.

---

[93]https://twitter.com/chuckgrassley/status/1047760081742434304?lang=en

[94]Erin Kelly, USA TODAY Published 10:23 a.m. ET Oct. 5, 2018 | Updated 4:32 p.m. ET Oct. 5, 2018 https://www.usatoday.com/story/news/politics /2018/10/05/fbi-report-kavanaugh-no-corroboration-allegations/1532476002/

[95]For more on the reactions of Republican and Democrats to the confidential FBI report see the AP Article: "Kavanaugh says he 'might have been too emotional' at hearing." By ALAN FRAM and LISA MASCARO October 5, 2018 https://www.apnews.com/7c36ea4fd38e43639cb6598f9a323bf6   These reactions are also found in the USA Today article https://www.usatoday.com/story/news/politics/2018/10/05/fbi-report-kavanaugh-no-corroboration-allegations/1532476002

10

Third Engagement:

Dividing Satan's Kingdom
Phase 2—Giving Commands

The previous chapter described the political events and revelations that took place during the suspenseful week before the full Senate vote would be taken on October 6, 2018. I have been very careful to note the exact time when the various events took place and when information was made public because events that occur in chronological time correspond to and interface with events taking place in the spiritual realm.

On the morning of October 4, before the results of the FBI became public that afternoon, the Holy Spirit fell upon me. The Lord revealed to me that a shift had taken place in the spiritual realm, that we were entering what may be called a kairos moment of opportunity for God's work. At the same time, we were entering the *hour of the power of darkness* when Satan was also at work. I could feel this change taking place and so could other intercessors.

Entering the Hour of the Power of Darkness

Let me explain the term *hour of the power of darkness* as it is important for intercessors to understand in order to cooperate with the Holy Spirit in defeating Satan's plans. This is the time when the conditions are optimal for Satan to work. The events leading up to Jesus being crucified were in just such a time.

When the temple guard came to arrest Jesus in the garden of Gethsemane, Jesus said, "Day after day when I was with you in the temple courts, you did not arrest me. But this is your hour, and that of the power of darkness!" (Luke 22:53)[96] *Hour* here is a different Greek word for time from *kairos*. *Chronos* means the type of time that is measured on a clock with hours, minutes and seconds, or on a calendar with days, weeks, and years. Only God the Father, Son and Holy Spirit, is Lord over time; He works outside of time. However, when the Holy Spirit enters into time, we experience this as *kairos,* or time that is fulfilled. Satan, however, works within the constraints of chronological time. The *hour of the power of darkness* is a time when the words and actions of Satan's human agents are demonically empowered, resulting in the furthering of Satan's plans on earth. In the biblical case, the result was Satan's Pyrrhic victory of the crucifixion of Jesus Christ.

In history, there are many examples of the *hour of the power of darkness* when actions by Satan's human agents connect with the working of demons and elicit human cooperation to accomplish Satan's purposes. When the right conditions are aligned for Satan to empower his demonized human agents, these actions amplify and multiply satanic darkness and advance Satan's evil plans on earth. Kristallnacht, "the night of broken glass," is an example of

---

[96]John 16:2-4 ASV contains another instance of Jesus using the same wording. "...but an hour is coming for everyone who kills you to think that he is offering service to God." And in verse 4, "...when their hour comes, you may remember that I told you of them."

this dynamic. On November 9-10, 1938, the Nazis in many German and Austrian cities went on a coordinated rampage attacking and killing Jews, destroying their shops and businesses, and burning synagogues. This took place in an *hour of the power of darkness* prepared for by Hitler's incendiary speeches and violent Nazi propaganda inciting a pervasive hatred of the Jewish people. These horrific actions were empowered by demons working in the hearts of those who cooperated in forming the stronghold of Nazism, contributing to an escalating cycle of evil culminating in the extermination of over six million men, woman, and children.

During the week when the reports were coming in vindicating Brett Kavanaugh and exposing the immoral tactics of the Democrats and Radical Left, I discerned that in the looming possibility of defeat, starting in the spiritual realm, Satan was stirring up some new trouble to derail the vote of the Senate on October 6th.

On earth, there was an uneasy calm in which it seemed some new devilry was in the making. It felt to me, and to other intercessors, that we had entered the hour of the power of darkness in which Satan's agents were plotting some actions that would be demonically empowered to completely derail the confirmation process and further stir up anarchy. I did not know what this would be. The opposition, especially the Radical Left, had already demonstrated that they were capable of using any means necessary to accomplish their goal of stopping the Kavanaugh nomination. Having cast off all moral constraints, and deceived by the Marxist/Hegelian religious conviction, anything seemed possible: mass protest, new allegations, terrorist attacks, even assassinations. Anything in their play book to stir anarchy which, according to their delusions, would birth the new perfect society, but in fact would only set in motion Satan's plans for greater evil.[97]

---

[97]The evidence suggests that there was a play book! It is radical leftist Saul Alinsky's *Rules for Radicals*. These 13 rules were deployed quite effectively by

On the morning of the 4th my prayer was, "Lord what are you calling me to do?" No answer came, yet the Spirit was upon me and prayed through me in tongues. This went on for several hours and was a season of sweet communion and refreshment in the presence of the Father, Son, and Holy Spirit. I would have enjoyed staying in this intimacy with God, but after a time He started to provide guidance. He was preparing me and the rest of the POTUS Cohort intercessors for a showdown with Satan's evil forces who were working to block the confirmation of Judge Kavanaugh. I suspected this battle would include my giving the command that Satan's kingdom be divided. But this would require more preparation of myself and those whom God was calling to be in unity of heart and mind in making the command. Frankly, I was reluctant to move forward with this as I knew it could be a dangerous provocation of high-level demonic spirits.

You Cannot be Neutral in a Showdown Between the Kingdom of God and the Empire of Satan

As I was praying into all of this, the Lord spoke to me again: He said, "You cannot be neutral in this contest between truth and lies." Then He asked a pointed question. He said, "Are you 100% convinced that it is my will, that Brett Kavanaugh is the one I have chosen for this position? Are you 100% convinced that he is telling the truth when he says that he is innocent of all the allegations of sexual misconduct? Or, are you hedging your bets?"

With this word I realized I had been hedging my bets. In my

Democrats and their allies in opposing the nomination. A complete analysis of these 13 rules and how they were deployed is beyond the scope of this book, but the intercessor must be aware of these tactics. I recommend the following as verification that these rules were being deployed: *How Democrats Are Using Saul Alinsky's Smear Tactics Against Brett Kavanaugh Chicago radical leftist Saul Alinsky's 13 rules for destroying conservatives are effective. The first step to challenging them is actually recognizing them.*
https://thefederalist.com/2018/09/14/democrats-using-saul-alinskys-smear-tactics-brett-kavanaugh/

attempt to be fair and evenhanded, I had started with the possibility that Judge Kavanaugh could have been guilty, and that Dr. Ford and the others were telling the truth. But as time went on, and I had carefully weighed the evidence available in the reports from the Senate Judiciary Committee and listened to Kavanaugh, to Dr. Ford, and the other accusers with my critical mind and heart, I had come to the conclusion that he was telling the truth. But I was waiting for the FBI report to be made public before I would fully commit myself to the fact that he was innocent and that everyone else, either intentionally or unintentionally, was lying.

In my dialogue with the Lord, I asked if I could have more time to make this decision once I heard the outcome of the FBI investigation. As reported in the last chapter, the FBI supplemental background check found no evidence to corroborate the allegations made by Dr. Ford or any of the other accusers. But on the morning of the 4th those results vindicating Kavanaugh were not yet public, or at least I was not aware of them.

The Lord spoke clearly and decisively, "No, you must decide NOW! as Satan has already launched his attacks and they must be resisted NOW! To wait until you have all the information you think you need will be too late, and this battle will be lost."

I struggled with this guidance to decide immediately and wondered why it was so important. Not as words this time, but as thoughts I am sure were coming from the Holy Spirit; I knew that we were in a battle between good and evil in which there could be no neutrality. I had to decide one way or the other. Otherwise I would not be able to join the battle of shaping God's future. I knew that I could not advance the Kingdom of God from the sidelines of neutrality or indecision. It occurred to me that this was the choice being presented to the Congress and to the nation. Would we as a nation go with truth or with lies? And that choice was being starkly presented in the one critical question, "Was Judge Kavanaugh telling the truth or was he lying when he said,

"This is a completely false allegation. I have never done anything like what the accuser describes—to her or to

149

anyone." "Because this never happened, I had no idea who was making this accusation until she identified herself yesterday.[98]

That was the stark choice being presented to me. Then the Lord said, "Do you think I could have bound the Devil in Hitler through my servant Rees Howells if he had harbored any areas of neutrality in this battle with evil?" From my study of the World War II intercessor, I knew that Rees Howells had had to make this decision that he was dealing with the Devil when dealing with Hitler before all the radical evils of Nazism in the Holocaust and the slaughter of millions had taken place.[99] The lesson I learned from the example of Rees Howells is that there can be no neutrality when fighting the Devil.

As I struggled with all this, I asked the Lord if there was anything that had taken place that would provide a reliable confirmation that Kavanaugh was telling the truth. The Lord answered, "Yes! He is a man of God, and would not lie to Me." With that there rushed back into my mind the extraordinary conclusion to the hearing when Senator John Kennedy, a Republican from Louisiana, asked the following questions:

---

[98]https://www.thedailybeast.com/kavanaugh-sexual-assault-accusations-completely-false

[99]It was in March, 1936 that Mr. Howells began to see clearly that Hitler was Satan's agent for preventing the gospel going to every creature. As he said later, "In fighting Hitler we have always said that we were not up against man, but the devil. Mussolini is a man, but Hitler is different. He can tell the day this 'spirit' came into him." For several years Mr. Howells stressed the fact that God must destroy him, if the vision of the Gospel to every creature was to be fulfilled. https://achristian.files.wordpress.com/2014/01/rees-howells_-intercessor-_-chapter-34-e28093-intercession-for-dunkirk.pdf

(This is my transcript of the video.)[100]

John Kennedy: "Do you believe in God?
Brett Kavanaugh: Yes, I do.
John Kennedy: "I am going to give you one last opportunity right here in front of God and country. I want you to look me in the eye. Are Dr. Ford's allegations true?
Brett Kavanaugh: They are not accurate as to me. I have not questioned that she may have been sexually assaulted at some point in her life by someone some place; but as to me, I have never done this, never! Done this to her or to anyone else. I have talked to you about what I was doing that summer of 1982, I am telling you I have never done this to anyone including her.
John Kennedy: "Are Miss Ramirez's allegations about you true?
Brett Kavanaugh: "Those are not. None of the witnesses in the room support that. If that had happened, it would have been the talk of campus in our freshman dorm. The NY Times reported last week that she was calling other classmates seeking to... well I am not going to characterize it... calling classmates last week, it just seemed very.... Lots of stuff there... it is not true, not true.
John Kennedy: "Are Miss Swetnick's allegations made by Mr. Avenatti about you true?
Brett Kavanaugh: Those are not true, never met her, do not know who she is, there is a letter released within two hours of that breaking yesterday from sixty people who knew me in high school, men and women, said... their words "nonsense" the whole thing, totally ridiculous.
John Kennedy: "None of these allegations are true?
Brett Kavanaugh: "Correct.
John Kennedy: "No doubt in your mind?"
Brett Kavanaugh: "Zero, 100% certain.

---

[100]https://youtu.be/7zVOkb3CdZO?t=32207

John Kennedy: "Not even a scintilla?
Brett Kavanaugh: "Not a scintilla, 100% certain, Senator."
John Kennedy: "You swear to God?"
Brett Kavanagh: "I swear to God."
John Kennedy: "That is all I have Judge."

I am convinced that Brett Kavanaugh is a Christian who believes in God and would not lie before God who knows all the secrets of the human heart and is our judge. This testimony along with all the other facts led me to conclude that, yes! Kavanaugh was telling the truth; and with that I gave up any areas of neutrality. I was then in 100% and ready to move forward with what my commander Jesus Christ would call me to do as part of His battle strategy.

The next guidance was very uncomfortable to me. It was, "You must call the intercessors to decide now whether they believe that Kavanaugh is telling the truth or not. And you must tell them to get ready to implement my command that Satan's Kingdom will be divided."

I shared with them in a video and in writing that I had decided that to be in this battle fully, that I could not be neutral, and so I had flung myself wholeheartedly into the prayer battle for what I believed was God's will to be accomplished, which was that Judge Brett Kavanaugh would take a seat on the Supreme Court. This is so that the battle to preserve the Judeo-Christian foundations of this nation may take another step toward victory. I told them that if it turned out that Brett Kavanaugh was lying to God and to the American people, then I would be the first to retract what I stated here. I told them that at least at the moment of decision, I would not have been found guilty of sitting on the sidelines; or by my unwillingness to commit 100%, to have actually been found to have played into Satan's hands in this battle for the soul of America.

I concluded with my opinion of what was at stake: "I fear that if we as individuals, as government leaders and as a nation, choose to believe a false witness instead of the truth sworn to before God by an innocent man and backed up by the six previous FBI background checks and reports, the conclusions of Rachel Mitchell that there was no case, then we as a government and as a nation have acquiesced to Satan plans for our own destruction. Those who are creating lies in order to destroy an innocent man and to impose their political agenda will come under the judgment of God."

I concluded in the video and in the letter, that they each had to decide for themselves whether or not Kavanaugh was telling the truth. Were they all in, or still equivocating, waiting for more information to come in? Until they were all in, it would not be safe for them to move forward into the next phase of the battle.

Needless to say, this created a lot of push back. Some intercessors were offended that they had to decide before all the information had come in from the FBI. Only a few, including JuleAnn and Jon, agreed and decided to make the decision to be all in. Looking back, I now realize that the Lord was doing a Gideon-type reduction of the prayer cohort in order to retain only those who could safely engage in the next phase of the battle.

The Strategy of Commanding Satan's Kingdom to be Divided

Let me explain this strategy of giving the command that Satan's Kingdom be divided. It is <u>not that we pray</u> for Satan's kingdom to be divided, <u>but</u> that at Jesus' instructions, <u>we give the command</u> that Satan's Kingdom is divided. When we do this in a kairos moment, the Holy Spirit uses our words to actually destroy the unity of Satan's command and control system that holds demons as well as their human agents in Satan's thrall. Satan's empire is held together by fear and hatred, and when this unity is divided, then it comes apart and the demons turn and devour each other. The result is that because of the breakdown in Satan's empire of evil, he is unable to carry out his plans that could have been accomplished in the *hour of the power of darkness.*[101]

The basis for this strategy is the words of Jesus given in Mark 3:24-27.

> If a kingdom is divided against itself, that kingdom will not be able to stand. If a house is divided against itself, that house will not be able to stand. And if Satan rises against himself and is divided, he is not able to stand and his end has come. But no one is able to enter a strong man's house and steal his property unless he first ties up the strong man. Then he can thoroughly plunder his house.

Only the Holy Spirit who knows the mind of Christ as well as the full complex interface between the human and demonic realms knows why and when to apply this tactic. But I could discern the reasons to divide Satan's kingdom in order to prepare the way for the Senate vote.

First, we felt that as it was a time of the *hour of the power of darkness,* anything that Satan's human agents would do would have an amplifying and reverberating effect in accomplishing Satan's plans.

Second, the margins were so slim that one or two people could make the difference between the confirmation failing or succeeding. So, we assumed that both Satan as well as the entire political machine of the opposition would focus on those few vulnerable Republicans who could be turned, and those Democratic senators who could defect. The social media, political, and spiritual pressure upon them appeared to be enormous.

Third, throughout the entire confirmation process, the opposition to confirming a judge recommended by Trump was

---

[101] I am indebted to Asher Intrater for this concept of giving the command that Satan's Kingdom is divided. From personal conversations with him at Revive Israel in Israel. Also, the biblical basis of this tactic is well described by Asher in his book *From Iraq to Armageddon: The Final Showdown Approaches*, pp. 150-152. (Destiny Image Incorporated, January 1, 2005. First published April 1, 2003.)

uniform and consistent. This consistency was found in the liberal press, in the protestors, and among the Democratic senators on the Judiciary Committee as well as among the rest of the Democratic senators. There were also several Republicans who were uncertain how they would vote. There seemed to me to be an invisible hand guiding the entire process, working out of a master playbook, coordinating this opposition to God's intentions of restoring the Supreme Court to its role of interpreting the US Constitution the way the founders intended.

On the human level I had no evidence to support the idea that there was a hidden, unified command structure in place. Rather, it was more like the conspiracy of shared opposition to and hatred of Donald Trump. It also seemed to be a conspiracy of shared liberal progressive ideals. The invisible hand guiding the process and bringing unity to all the different parties was, I was sure, Satan. He and his demonic forces had found an open door into many in the Democratic Party and those protesters who had been captivated by an ideology that basically rejects God and promotes agendas clearly against our Judeo-Christian values—values which are based on the revelation of the Bible, the Word of God. This unified opposition must be broken in the human realm, but this can only take place if it is first broken in the spiritual realm. Therefore, I believed God was calling us to give this command to divide Satan's Kingdom. This would enable the human actors in the drama to do their part of breaking through.

Giving this command is not something one does lightly or without the explicit command of Jesus Christ. Each time I have acted on this guidance, there have been intense demonic counter attacks. It is a form of calling out Satan. A throwing down the gauntlet. I have seen people destroyed for doing this, and frankly have nearly been so myself.

Adding the Call to Praise

On Friday morning about 9 o'clock on October 5, I was directed by the Holy Spirit to make a video praying these commands. A great urgency came over me that this had to be done right then. It could not wait even for a second cup of morning tea! This was the day that the Senate would decide whether or not to close debate, which was necessary if the vote on Kavanaugh's confirmation was to take place on the 6th.

As I was setting up the video camera and getting ready to pray in obedience to Jesus Christ, an intercessor who did not know I was about to make this video, called on my mobile phone with strong guidance, urging me to direct intercessors to pray 2 Chronicles 20:20-23.

(19)   Then some Levites, from the Kohathites and Korahites, got up and loudly praised the LORD God of Israel. (20) Early the next morning they marched out to the Desert of Tekoa. When they were ready to march, Jehoshaphat stood up and said: "Listen to me, you people of Judah and residents of Jerusalem! Trust in the LORD your God and you will be safe! Trust in the message of his prophets and you will win." (21) He met with the people and appointed musicians to play before the LORD and praise his majestic splendor. As they marched ahead of the warriors they said: "Give thanks to the LORD, for his loyal love endures." (22) When they began to shout and praise, the LORD suddenly attacked the Ammonites, Moabites, and men from Mount Seir who were invading Judah, and they were defeated. (23) The Ammonites and Moabites attacked the men from Mount Seir and annihilated them. When they had finished off the men of Seir, they attacked and destroyed one another.

This seemed like a lot to read on the video, but I witnessed to it that the timing and the call to praise was from the Lord. So I added the reading of these verses and the call to praise God for His victory to the video. I notified a few intercessors, including those who had communicated to me that they were all in, that I was moving into this dangerous engagement with the powers and principalities. I asked that they back me up.

Giving the Commands Over Video

So in my living room at home, sitting in front of the video camera with the studio lights on, I gave a short summary of this strategy. I asked all those who listened to the video to please join me if, and only if, they were prompted by the Holy Spirit to join me, in commanding that Satan's empire of wickedness was divided.[102] Unlike the battle in the heavenlies at the Royal Gorge Lookout point, this was not dramatic at all, but simply declaring out loud the following commands: (These are not verbatim from the video which were led by the Holy Spirit specifically for that moment. These are more generic and represent the pattern of this type of command.)

- "In the name of Jesus Christ, Son of the living God, I call to attention all in the demonic realm and those legions of Hell who are working against God's sovereign plan to place Brett Kavanaugh, an "originalist judge" a man of God, on the Supreme Court of the US."

- "In the name of Jesus Christ, I command that portion of the empire of Satan that is over the US Capital is divided."

- "In the strong and mighty name of Jesus Christ who defeated you by His blood on the Cross, I bind you Satan and any other "strongmen' (high-level evil spirits) who are in control over the Capital of the United States."

---

[102]You can view the video that I sent to a few intercessors here: https://vimeo.com/293632151

- "By the authority of Jesus Christ, I cut off your influence over those human beings whom you have deceived or confused to follow your plans."

- "In the Name of Jesus Christ, the Alpha and the Omega, I command that your schemes for evil will be confused and come to naught."

I then read 2 Chronicles 20:19-23 and offered up praise and thanksgiving for what in faith I believed God was doing.

As I prayed this in front of the video camera, I could see into the demonic realm with the eyes of the Spirit. Confusion was breaking loose; demons were turning against each other. On earth I could see with the eyes of the Spirit that the fog of confusion and deception that seemed to have settled over Congress was being pierced by the light of God's presence, making room for clear thinking and reasoned debate. As I prayed, I felt demons coming against me. I felt sick, and waves of confusion went over me. But as I persisted praying in the Spirit and moving into praise, the attacks lifted and a deep peace of having fulfilled what the Lord told me to do came over me.

I immediately worked to edit and render the video clip and send it off by e-mail to that very small group of intercessors who had joined me in this prayer work, those who were "all in," and those on the POTUS network.

Around 50 people viewed the video that morning. That evening I received a text message report from JuleAnn. The Holy Spirit had led her to engage with me in this phase of the battle.

> Brad,
>
> I've been in and out of engagement all day [Friday October 5th] — I'm at the Dunamis Project Equipping Event on the Gifts of the Holy Spirit in NJ—the LORD called me out of teaching during morning session today. As soon as I saw this video delivered to my email —I excused myself to listen—as I was

watching, I could "hear" hissing, with rage and terror coming from hordes of demons that were attempting to press in. Physically I'm experiencing sharp pains in my neck—on the right side. I sense this was the enemy pushing back as it started when I heard the LORD nudge me to leave the teaching session and go to my room to pray (this was roughly around 10:30-11 AM this morning).

The pain has only worsened. I have also been actively called to pray protection over the Kavanaughs, but also over you and your family and PRMI. I've been asking the LORD to awaken intercessors to step into the gap. I'm now going to step into the act of prophetic worship with the participants here at the Dunamis event as you suggest in the video.

May the Shalom of our LORD Jesus Christ envelope you, JuleAnn

By joining me in praying the commands that Satan's empire be divided, JuleAnn had fulfilled Jesus' conditions for the Father to answer our prayers.

"I tell you the truth, whatever you bind on earth will have been bound in heaven, and whatever you release on earth will have been released in heaven. (19) Again, I tell you the truth, if two of you on earth agree about whatever you ask, my Father in heaven will do it for you. (20) For where two or three are assembled in my name, I am there among them." (Matthew 18:18-20)

After I had released the video praying these commands and in faith offering praise, I awaited further directions from the Lord. In faith I expected that something would soon take place on the Senate floor as the result of Satan's kingdom being divided in the spiritual realm. I did not have long to wait.

The Speech by Susan Collins

Friday the 5th was a day filled with tension while the entire Senate was debating whether or not to confirm Brett Kavanaugh to the Supreme Court. According to Senate rules, a vote must be taken to close debate, then 24 hours later a vote may be taken. No doubt there were many backroom conversations going on. This is all part of the normal political process. But I had no way of knowing what was taking place in the human realm. My role had been entirely in the spiritual realm. However, I was certain that if our work and the battles in the spiritual realm had had any effect, we would see this in whether the senators voted to close debate and move toward a vote.

Hanging in the balance were the votes of several undecided Republicans, one of whom was Susan Collins of Maine. Late Friday afternoon, on October 5th, she gave an amazing speech, laying out our democratic foundations such as due process and innocent until proven guilty. At the end of the speech, after holding everyone in suspense for nearly forty-five minutes, she announced that she would vote for Kavanaugh to be confirmed to the Supreme Court.

Here is the announcement and a summary from CNN:

Washington (CNN)
Republican Sen. Susan Collins said on Friday that she plans to support Brett Kavanaugh's nomination to the Supreme Court, an announcement that has put the nomination on track for confirmation.

"I will vote to confirm Judge Kavanaugh," the Maine senator said in a Senate floor speech that lasted for more than 40 minutes.

With Collins planning to vote for Kavanaugh, it appears that Senate Republicans have the votes needed for final confirmation. Within moments of her announcement, Democratic Sen. Joe Manchin of West Virginia announced he would support Kavanaugh, shoring up enough votes to confirm his nomination.

In a sign of how tense the fight over the nomination had

become, just before Collins had a chance to give her speech, chants of "Show up for Maine women, vote no" broke out in the Senate chamber.

Collins said that she believes that Christine Blasey Ford, who testified last week before the Senate Judiciary Committee that Kavanaugh sexually assaulted her in the early 1980s, "is a survivor of a sexual assault and that this trauma has upended her life."

But, she argued that ultimately the allegation was not corroborated.

"The four witnesses she named could not corroborate any of the events of that evening gathering where she says the assault occurred," she said. Kavanaugh himself has vehemently denied the allegation.

"I do not believe that these charges can fairly prevent Judge Kavanaugh from serving on the court," the senator concluded.[103]

There was much more to the speech, and I recommend that you listen to it and read the transcript.[104] I believe her speech cut through all the deception and exposed the truth. She was the deciding factor in having enough votes to close debate.

Often a vote like this to close debate is an indication of how the senators will vote, but not always. So, this was a good indication that Judge Kavanaugh might be confirmed.[105] However, I could not relax, and most of the night still had the Holy Spirit praying through me.

---

[103]https://www.cnn.com/2018/10/05/politics/collins-kavanaugh-vote-nomination-announcement/index.html

[104]Read the full transcript of Sen. Collins's speech announcing she'll vote to confirm Brett Kavanaugh. "He has been an exemplary public servant, judge, teacher, coach, husband, and father." By Stavros Agorakis Oct 5, 2018, 5:50pm EDT https://www.vox.com/2018/10/5/17943276/susan-collins-speech-transcript-full-text-kavanaugh-vote Or view the video here: https://www.youtube.com/watch?v=iXzzmjgyO9k

[105]https://www.wsj.com/articles/senators-prepare-for-kavanaugh-vote-with-gop-confident-1538745278

Then the next morning Laura and I loaded our car and headed off for a week of beach vacation which was desperately needed. On the five-hour trip through South Carolina, the Holy Spirit keep praying through me and we kept switching on the radio and checking e-mail to see what was taking place on the Senate floor. As we pulled into the rental apartment at North Myrtle Beach, we heard the news.

"The Senate confirmed Brett Kavanaugh to the Supreme Court on Saturday in a 50-48 vote, with Vice President Mike Pence presiding over the vote that is expected to cement a conservative majority on the nation's highest court for decades to come."[106]

We rejoiced! Then the Holy Spirit lifted from me, and for the first time since the battle began, I started to relax.

Witches gather to Curse Brett Kavanaugh

We had a wonderful week at the beach in rest and recovery. I had the space to start reflecting upon the extraordinary prayer battle that we had just been through. We were on our way back from the beach on October 15 when Jon Gurley, the intercessor who is constantly in touch with the news, texted me the following article from the Guardian:

Cursed: witches are planning a public hexing of Brett Kavanaugh—The planned ceremony has angered Fox News and right-wing commentators, which is exactly the point says the

---

[106]https://www.google.com/search?q=what+was+the+final+vote+count +for+kavanaugh&oq=What+was+the+final+vote+for+Kavnaugh+&aqs=chrome. 2.69i57j0l2.17481j0j8&sourceid=chrome&ie=UTF-8

organizer.[107]

Apparently, having lost the battle through our democratic process, the Devil with his human allies had shifted the tactics to witchcraft. The very same thing had happened when failing to prevent Donald Trump from being elected as President of the United States—the witch covens and occultists moved into the monthly rituals of cursing Trump and all who supported him. While some may see this as a joke, it is a very serious matter to intentionally invoke demonic powers. Tucker Carlson of Fox News named this danger and linked it to other evils like the abortion industry. He was, of course, mocked by the liberal media.[108] However, he is right! It is dangerous to invoke the Devil. He is always ready to take advantage of such invitations.

I discussed this news with Rev. Martin Boardman, our PRMI prayer mobilizer, after which he sent out a notice to the POTUS Prayer Network. We invited the intercessors to pray, "Lord, are you calling us to engage in what looks like the next phase of this battle?" As we were waiting for their discernment, an intercessor who is Roman Catholic sent us the following note:

BLOGS | OCT. 17, 2018 Patti Armstrong - Exorcist and Catholics Respond to Curse Against Kavanaugh: Word is spreading to pray and fast, not just for the protection of Kavanaugh, but for those who wish him harm.[109]

As I read this article, I felt the Holy Spirit saying to me, "No, this is not your battle! I am calling another team to engage this one."

---

[107] https://www.theguardian.com/us-news/2018/oct/15/witches-public-hexing-brett-kavanaugh

[108] http://insider.foxnews.com/2018/10/12/brett-kavanaugh-be-hexed-witches-brooklyn-new-york-liberal-sherpa-says

[109] http://www.ncregister.com/blog/armstrong/exorcist-and-catholics-respond-to-curse-against-kavanaugh

Frankly this was a great relief! As I thought about it, I realized the great wisdom in the Lord's battle plan. He had shifted this phase of the war to those who have the authority to step into the gap for Kavanaugh and his family who are Roman Catholic.

God's army of intercessors has many units, and Jesus deploys them according to His own master plan. It was very exciting to watch this hand-off to another team of intercessors who were called to take the lead in this phase of the battle.

This concludes the in-depth story and after-action reviews of the three prayer engagements that we went through as we cooperated with the Holy Spirit in advancing God's Kingdom purposes in placing an originalist judge, Judge Brett Kavanaugh, onto the US Supreme Court.

I will not be adding the after-action review for this last engagement. We were all scattered by this time and were called into other prayer battles, and so we were not able to do one. However, I have expanded this chapter to include observations and explanations that normally would have been covered in an AAR.

In the next chapter I will summarize the timeless lessons for intercessors and spiritual warriors that we gleaned from this extraordinary prayer battle.

11

Summary of the Timeless Lessons for Prayer Warriors

This chapter is an after-action review of the entire battle for the confirmation of Judge Kavanaugh. My purpose is to draw out and highlight nine timeless lessons that apply to future battles intercessors will face in warfare with Satan, a war that will finally end in complete victory when Jesus Christ returns in glory.

This summary after-action review will explicitly reveal those behind-the-scenes dynamics of cooperating with the Holy Spirit that directed intercessors in the deployment of tactics which the Lord used to defeat Satan's schemes and advance God's Kingdom plans.

Lesson # 1 - Concerts of Prayer Consist of Many Networks of Intercessors

Each prayer engagement revealed the role of different groups of intercessors whom the Holy Spirit deployed into the battle. The largest grouping is the pervasive on-going work of the Holy Spirit praying through all those of biblical faith. This includes the prayers of Jews and Christians crying out to the One True God revealed in the Old and New Testaments. This general work of prayer is expressed specifically in the Jewish Amidah,[110] "You are eternally mighty, Lord. You give life to the dead and have great power to save..."[111] It is also embodied in Yeshua/Jesus' direction that we pray, "...may your kingdom come, may your will be done on earth as it is in heaven." (Matthew 6:10-11) The general work of prayer also includes the prayers of those whom the Bible identifies as those who "fear God" and follow the dictates of the conscience, and show that the "work of the Torah is written in their hearts." (Romans 2:14-16 TLV)[112] This could include those of many different faiths and of no formal religious faith.

From this pervasive prayer, the Lord has conducted all through history what may be identified as "concerts of prayer." These arise from waves or pulses of the Holy Spirit through which the Kingdom of God is advanced and the Great Commission is fulfilled. Examples are the prayer movements that preceded the great outpouring of the Holy Spirit from 1890 to 1910. This included the D.L. Moody and R.A. Torrey revivals in the English-speaking world, the Welsh revival, the Korean revival, and others. A more recent example is the 1960-1980s outpouring of the Holy Spirit in the Charismatic renewal. Such concerts of prayer may also take place as God's

---

[110] The Amidah (Hebrew: תפילת העמידה, Tefilat HaAmidah, "The Standing Prayer") also called the Shemoneh Esreh (שמנה עשרה,) is the central prayer of the Jewish liturgy. This prayer, among others, is found in the Siddur, the traditional Jewish prayer book. Due to its importance, it is simply called hatefila (תפילה,) "prayer") in rabbinic literature. [1] https://en.wikipedia.org /wiki/Amidah

[111] *The Koren Siddur*, Korn Publishers Jerusalem, Orthodox Union (2013) p. 480.

[112] Romans 2:14-16 TLV For when Gentiles, who do not have the Torah, do by nature the things of the Torah, they are a law to themselves even though they do not have the Torah. (15) They show that the work of the Torah is written in their hearts, their conscience bearing witness and their thoughts switching between accusing or defending them (16) on the day when God judges the secrets of men according to my Good News through Messiah Yeshua.

response to overcoming threats to His Kingdom from Satan's demonic strongholds.

As I stated in the opening chapter giving the spiritual context of the confirmation battle, I believe that we are presently in another major movement of the Holy Spirit which may be identified as the westward blowing wind of the Spirit that began in Jerusalem with Pentecost and is now returning to Jerusalem. This consists of four distinct tributaries or waves of the Holy Spirit: 1.) The Jews returning to the land of Israel and to faith in Yeshua the Messiah. 2.) The back to Jerusalem Movement among those of Confucian culture—Koreans, Japanese, and Chinese taking the Gospel of Jesus Christ along the Silk Road through the heartlands of Islam. 3.) An awakening in the Western world of Roman Catholics, Protestants, and Pentecostals for fulfilling the Great Commission. 4.) A wind of the Holy Spirit blowing in the "house of Islam" bringing Muslims to faith in Jesus Christ.[113]

I believe the work of prayer to confirm Judge Kavanaugh to the Supreme Court is but one skirmish in this third great wave of the Holy Spirit in the Western world.

Within this third wave this battle is the result of a concert of prayer through which God is defeating Satan's plans to prevent the United States, Canada, and the United Kingdom from fulfilling their holy destiny of providing freedom and liberty to the nations, protecting Israel, and creating the context for those of biblical faith to have the freedom and resources to take part in the global advancement of the Kingdom of God.

Each concert of prayer includes specific prayer networks consisting of many hundreds, even thousands of intercessors. In some cases, such as major revivals or global calamities like World War II, millions of intercessors may be involved. In the Kavanaugh

---

[113] I describe these four great waves of the Holy Spirit as the conclusion of my book *A Prayer Strategy for the Victory of Jesus Christ*: *Defeating the Demonic Strongholds of ISIS and Radical Islam* (PRMI Exousia Press, 2018.)

confirmation battle, there were no doubt many active prayer networks including hundreds, and possibility thousands, of intercessors. PRMI intercessors, however, were personally connected with only a few of these networks. Others were the Jerusalem Prayer Tower located in Jerusalem, Israel,[114] the POTUS Shield,[115] and Intercessors for America.[116] PRMI's networks consist of the hundreds of people on the Discerning the Times mailing list. But this group was reduced to about fifty who were specifically called to pray for President Trump and the confirmation of Brett Kavanaugh to the US Supreme Court.

A timeless principle of such concerts of prayer is that the Holy Spirit is working on earth through vast networks of intercessors under the command and direction of Jesus Christ. Communications between these networks are now facilitated by the internet. But the important truth is, it is Jesus Christ through the Holy Spirit who is the conductor of this great concert. He guides each network and even each individual intercessor to fulfill their unique and specific roles.

Another major lesson from this is that we will not fully understand the particular prayer battle that we are called to engage in unless we can see it in the larger context of God's master plans for advancing the Kingdom and Satan's opposition. In the big picture of God's Kingdom, this battle to confirm Kavanaugh (an originalist judge to the US Supreme Court) is part of a much larger move of the Holy Spirit.

Lesson # 2 - The "Gideon Effect"

In the PRMI prayer network, we experienced the Holy Spirit calling smaller and smaller groupings of intercessors into what we have called "prayer cohorts." Usually the optimal size for a cohort

---

[114]https://jerusalemprayertower.org/

[115] https://www.potusshield.org/

[116] https://www.ifapray.org/

is seven people. However, in two engagements with high-level demons in the heavenlies, the cohort was reduced even further to just two of us, and at one point to just one person when I went up the mountain alone.

I have called this narrowing of fewer and fewer intercessors the "Gideon Effect" after the account of Gideon in Judges 7. The Lord reduced Gideon's army from 32,000 men to only 300 while the more numerous enemy "covered the valley like a swarm of locusts, whose camels could not be counted; they were as innumerable as the sand on the seashore." This army was decisively defeated, not by human power and might, but by the hand of the Lord. (Judges 7:12) Reducing Gideon's army to only three hundred was necessary to demonstrate that it was the Lord who won the victory. This battle also reveals how a smaller number of just the right men were needed to cooperate with Gideon in order to implement the Lord's unconventional battle strategy.

A similar dynamic took place when the Lord continually called us into smaller and smaller units in the different phases of the engagement. This was done so He could receive all the glory by having just the few people He needed at each phase to cooperate with Him.

It is easier for smaller groupings of intercessors to meet Jesus' criteria for cooperating with Him in prayer to advance His Father's kingdom. These criteria are:

- A Relationship with Jesus— John 15:4-5, 7-8, I John 5:14-15
- Praying According to God's Will— I John 5:14-15:
- Asking and Receiving in Faith— Mark 11:22-24, Matthew 17:20-21
- Forgiveness—Mark 11:25
- Praying in The Name of Jesus— John 14:12-14, Acts 3:1-10
- Praying in Agreement—Matthew 18:19-20
- Persistence—Luke 11:8
- Praying with Authority in Christ for Binding and Loosing— Matthew 18:18, Mark 3:13, John 20:23

Take for instance the requirement for agreement in prayer. Jesus knows our sinful natures and how effective Satan is in dividing us into factions, so He sets the bar rather low. Just two or three are needed!

"Again, I tell you the truth, if two of you on earth agree about whatever you ask, my Father in heaven will do it for you. For where two or three are assembled in my name, I am there among them." (Matthew 18:19-20)

The larger the group, the greater the challenge to build agreement in the details required for effective intercession.

This principle was vividly illustrated when the Lord prepared us to command Satan's kingdom be divided. The means the Lord used to determine our level of agreement as a cohort was in forcing the POTUS intercessors to decide whether or not they 100% believed Brett Kavanaugh was telling the truth, even before the conclusions of the FBI supplemental background check had been announced. Only JuleAnn called to say she was 100% in and agreed with me in prayer. During the extended prayer battle, the Lord used other means to reduce us into smaller teams. For instance, during the September 27th hearings in which both Dr. Ford and Judge Kavanaugh were to testify, the Lord called a small group of intercessors out from the larger group to form a cohort. He did this by directing some to stay in the room and cover the meeting, and some to leave the meeting to go to another location to specifically pray for the hearing. Notice, however, that the smaller units were not replacing the larger prayer networks which remained in full operation, fulfilling their role in God's master battle strategy. I do not know whether the Lord used a similar strategy of calling forth these smaller focused groups in other networks. I suspect He did.

We must be careful not to make the means the Lord used to reduce the number of intercessors into a rule that is normative for all. Requiring cohort members to always agree that someone is telling the truth before needed information is received would be just as ridiculous as taking the army of Israel to streams of water before each battle to select troops for combat according to how they took a drink. The point is that we need to listen to the Lord and let Him do the selection of whom is called into the smaller groups. That is the timeless principle, not the means He chooses to accomplish the reduction in numbers.

A danger to avoid is placing undue focus on the small cohort or the one or two intercessors battling high-level demons in the heavenlies. We must remember that each grouping of intercessors has a critical role in the Lord's battle strategy. The danger is to focus on the intercessor alone on the mountain. For the one called alone into heavenly battle, the temptation is to fall into spiritual pride by thinking they are the only one that matters in the Father's vast concert of prayer. That attitude is the surest way to be removed from the role of an intercessor.

The timeless lesson learned is that God works through different groupings of intercessors from the large network down to the small cohort and even to the single intercessor. All need to be affirmed and equipped in their different but interconnected roles, and all are needed to defeat Satan's schemes and to advance the Kingdom of God.

Lesson # 3 - The Right Tactic Must be Applied at the Right Time

The tactics of intercession and spiritual warfare are relatively few: piercing the cloaking, binding Satan, speaking prophetic words, breaking curses, commanding Satan's kingdom to be divided, moving into praise, and so forth. Their effectiveness comes not from any inherent power in us or the tactic itself. Rather, these actions are offered to the Holy Spirit at precisely the right time and in the sequence of His maneuvers either against Satan or as the actions needed to further the Father's plans. Repeatedly during these engagements, the Holy Spirit would tell us He needed us to act on the guidance within a precise, often short time frame. For instance, when I was given guidance to make the video in which to give the commands dividing Satan's Kingdom, it had to be done right then. I did not even have time to get another cup of tea. If I had delayed launching these tactics for even a few minutes, the video would not have reached the intercessors in time for them to fit into the sequence of God's actions which were intended to impact what Satan was doing in the spiritual realm and among the senators' deliberations, hearts, and minds. The Lord knows what is taking place in all these interconnected dimensions; and from His vantage point, He guides us in the actions He needs us to take to fit precisely into the implementing of the master strategy.

This essential timing takes place within the dynamic of cooperating with the Holy Spirit in what we call *kairos moments of opportunity*. These are moments in which our human actions and words function within the conditions prepared for by the Holy Spirit. An example of this dynamic is the miracle of Jesus raising Lazarus from the dead in John 11. The miracle took place when Jesus Christ shouted out the command, "Lazarus, come out!" But for this command to connect with the working of the Holy Spirit to raise the man to life after being dead four days, a series of perfectly timed actions by Jesus and Martha were required. To give the command, "Lazarus, Come out," Jesus first had to arrive at Bethany, Martha had to confess that she believed that Jesus was the Messiah, the Resurrection and the Life, her faith needed to be clothed in the obedience of ordering the stone to be rolled away, and Jesus needed to look up to heaven and affirm that He always received guidance from the Father. When all these steps were completed, the command connected with the empowering work of the Holy Spirit, and the miracle then took place—the dead man came out alive!

If Jesus' command for Lazarus to come out of the tomb had been given out of sequence and without the timing of these preparatory events, the command would have been void of the Holy Spirit's power and Lazarus would have remained dead in the tomb.

The timeless lesson for the intercessor is that this dynamic of cooperating with the Holy Spirit is a complex dance in which each step, as well as the timing of each step, matters. To get this right, we must listen to the Holy Spirit and discern the guidance we receive for what action to take and the timing of when to act.

When our actions are in synch with God's actions, then the tactics of intercession and spiritual warfare are empowered by the Holy Spirit to accomplish God's kingdom plans. In the Kavanaugh confirmation process, despite well-coordinated, ferocious human and demonic opposition, an originalist Judge was seated on the Supreme Court. This action fulfilled one step in God's master battle plan of setting back Satan's scheme of replacing American's foundational Judeo-Christian values with the deceptions of Marxist ideology. This in turn was a part of the third great wave of the Holy Spirit bringing awakening to the Western world.

Lesson # 4 - The Dynamic Between the Roles of Moses the Intercessor and Joshua the Warrior

By describing the prayer engagements and the after-action reviews that followed, we have noted the various ways that God answered our prayers: The Republican senators on the Judiciary Committee voted to approve Judge Kavanaugh with the condition that a supplemental FBI background check be conducted before the final vote by the full Senate. The FBI discovered no evidence corroborating any of the allegations. Another answer to prayer was Senator Susan Collins making a powerful speech supporting the confirmation that most likely persuaded some others to vote for the confirmation.

The skeptic may ask, "What did any of that have to do with prayer? Was that not the result of the deal making of senators on the Committee, or the natural outcome of human decision making?" I would have to answer, "The results that were consistent with God's Kingdom purposes were evidence of God working through the interface between the intercessors and those senators on the Committee." To explain this dynamic, I must introduce to you a paradigm that I have found most helpful for understanding how God has chosen to work in the world.

I have already used the story of the battle of Amalek in Exodus 17:8-16 to explain the different roles of Moses, Aaron, and Hur within a prayer cohort. We must now return to this story to draw another timeless lesson out of the complex relationship between God's actions and our actions.

In summary, at a place called Rephidim, the army of Amalek came out to fight the people of Israel, blocking their journey to the Mountain of God. The Lord gave Moses the plan for battle. Moses, Aaron, and Hur were to go up on the hilltop to do the work of prayer. Meanwhile, Joshua and his army were to fight the army of the Amalekites in the valley below. Whenever Moses raised his staff (the symbol of divine authority granted to him), the Israelites prevailed in battle; but when Moses grew weary and let down his staff, the army of Amalek started to win. So, Moses sat on a rock with both Aaron and Hur holding up his arms and the staff of God until the sun went down and Joshua's army was victorious.

This battle illustrates the dynamic interrelationship between the Holy Spirit working within Moses, Aaron and Hur's roles of intercessors in the spiritual realm, and the Spirit accomplishing those prayers through the roles of Joshua and his army on the battlefield. Within this complex relationship, we see Satan's plans defeated and God's Kingdom work taking place. Both Moses and Joshua are warriors—Moses in the spiritual realm with spiritual weapons, and Joshua in the human realm with swords, spears and slings. Each had weapons suitable to defeat enemies similarly armed. Together they defeated the spiritual and human powers who were blocking fulfillment of God's redemptive plans of bringing the people of Israel to their world changing rendezvous with God on Mount Sinai. If either had stopped doing what they were called to do, the battle would have been lost and God's plans thwarted.

We find this very same dynamic and interface taking place between the intercessors and those human actors working in accord with God's purposes in the confirmation battle for Judge Kavanaugh. Throughout these pages the human actors, the Joshua workers on the ground, have been identified by name. To recall a few: God answered prayers to pierce the cloaking and reveal what was really taking place with the protesters through the young reporter Jon Brown. He exposed the fact that protesters were being paid.   Another key human actor, Rachel Mitchell, answered our prayers for piercing the cloaking by exposing what was taking place with her careful questioning of both Dr. Ford and Judge Kavanaugh.   Lindsey Graham emerged as a fiery orator, naming the true evil actions of some of the Democrats and encouraging Judge Kavanaugh by saying he had been through hell, declaring he deserved to be on the Supreme Court, and rallying the Republican senators to stand firm. The chairman of the committee, Senator Chuck Grassley, had to make wise decisions and manage the debate, knowing how to respond to the allegations. Then there was Judge Kavanaugh who had to run the gauntlet of relentless questioning and false allegations hurled at him from hostile senators.   The other Republican senators had to resist the extraordinary social and media pressure put on them to oppose the nomination.   Susan Collins crafted and delivered an excellent speech giving the reasons for her decision to vote to approve Kavanaugh.

All these actions were linked to the actions and prayers of intercessors just as Joshua's and the army's actions on the battlefield were linked to Moses', Aaron's and Hur's actions on the hill top in the spiritual realm.   The actions and words of an entire cast of human actors were the means through whom the prayers of intercessors were being implemented. There were battles in the heavenlies between angels and demons that were related to our prayers; but on earth, these prayers were answered by God through this cast of human actors who were enabled to make decisions and speak words that were consistent with His plans to uphold the Judeo-Christian values foundation of the United States. This is the key lesson: victory is a *both-and dynamic of prayer and faithful human actions.*

The timeless lesson for intercessors is the dynamic between their Moses work of prayer and the Joshua human actors. This requires our full engagement in praying for the Joshua workers through whom God is working. Practically speaking, the intercessor's call into the battle for the soul of America involves fulfilling the mandate given to us by Paul:

First of all, then, I urge that requests, prayers, intercessions, and thanks be offered on behalf of all people, (2) even for kings and all who are in authority, that we may lead a peaceful and quiet life in all godliness and dignity. (3) Such prayer for all is good and welcomed before God our Savior, (4) since he wants all people to be saved and to come to a knowledge of the truth. (1 Timothy 2:1-4)

Such prayer is not about playing politics, but in recognizing that our work as intercessors must be connected to and in the dynamic of cooperating with those whom God has given authority in government and society, and through whom He is working out His purposes in the nations of the world.

Lesson # 5 Do not Underestimate the Enemy

Throughout this book we have mentioned that we are up against Satan and the demonic spirits working through both individuals as well as through human social organizations that are intermingled with demonic entries. This prayer battle has led us to affirm without reservation that Satan and the power of evil and death were defeated on the Cross of Jesus Christ. (Colossians 2:15) We have again and again expressed in this battle the authority that Jesus Christ has given us over demons. (Luke 10:19) This authority that we have in Christ is real, and Jesus is the victor!

However, our experiences in this prayer battle demonstrate that the Devil not only has a large number of demons under his command, but uses humans who have bought into his lies and are under his influence. He marshals his forces for every battle, ambushes at opportune times, scrambles our communications, attacks with irrational fears, images, thoughts, accusations of past sins, and confusion. He tries to prevent a team as well as individuals from fulfilling their assignments.

The timeless lesson from these encounters with Satan is that we must not underestimate his cruelty or cunning or power. Nor can we presume to call out powerful demons without the direct leading of the Holy Spirit after we have met the conditions of careful preparation for such battles.

Lesson # 6 - The Important Role of the After-Action Review

Our role of cooperating with the Holy Spirit is a dynamic process requiring constant adaptation to our wily foe, who aggressively and with maniacal creativity, adjusts his tactics to counter any and all actions led by the Holy Spirit. Responding to the ever-changing circumstances of this battle requires that both intercessors and prayer teams be in a constant learning mode, perfecting their cooperation with the Holy Spirit and one another. The timeless lesson for intercessors is that the after-action review provides an optimal context for this constant learning and adaptation to take place. Victory in the war of advancing the Kingdom of God over Satan's empire of evil depends upon many factors. Among them are intercessors and prayer groups who rigorously implement the practice of after-action reviews after each engagement. Without this opportunity for learning, they will be apt to apply tactics and ways of prayer by rote rather than at the direction of Jesus Christ. This will render their prayers ineffective because they will not be in sync with what the Holy Spirit is doing in the engagement. This results in intercessors simply being irrelevant to the great movements of God's kingdom; giving the impression that prayer doesn't work which further discourages the church from praying. Worse than this, ineffective prayer is a way of insuring that Satan's intentions for evil prevail for longer periods, causing more wreckage, suffering, and tragedy to humanity than necessary.

Lesson # 7 - Offering the Guidance You Receive

Another timeless lesson that I have assumed throughout this book, but must be named, is the importance of all participants in the prayer battle offering the guidance they receive to the group, no matter how small or insignificant it may seem.

This relates to the importance of each person having a role and being faithful to it in prayer battles. We have repeatedly found that though a leader in the Moses role of intercession is on point, he or she does not receive all the guidance needed, nor is able to analyze and discern all the information coming in. This is the shared role of the extended prayer team. Together they must receive and then analyze the intel from both the natural and the spiritual realms. Each piece of information is vital to the big picture, giving a more complete understanding of what the Holy Spirit is calling each person involved to offer to the discernment process. It is often like putting together a jigsaw puzzle; each piece counts in completing the entire puzzle. And any one of us may have a crucial piece. To cite an example already given, after having been confirmed by the entire Senate, covens of witches and occultists launched a campaign of cursing Judge Kavanaugh. We were all seeking guidance about whether Jesus was calling PRMI intercessors into this next engagement. It did look like we would be, as we had been called into countering these witchcraft curses when they were made against newly elected President Trump. When a Roman Catholic individual noticed an article in her Catholic publication, she got the nudge to send it to the discernment team. This was just the piece of intel needed to complete the big picture of what God was doing. He was calling others to this engagement, not us.

The lesson is that each team member is of value and must add their bit of information to enable the cohort to collectively discern what the Devil is doing and how the Holy Spirit is leading. So do not hold back! Even if you think what you are getting is irrelevant or insignificant or implausible, it may be just the piece of intel that completes the puzzle, exposing Satan's stratagems or the Holy

Spirit's guidance.

Lesson # 8 - The Role of Relationships in the Cohort and with Jesus

The importance of relationships among the members of the cohort and prayer network has been mentioned throughout this book. The timeless lesson for intercessors and spiritual warriors is that the Holy Spirit works through the web of relationships among the members of the network or cohort. If a committed prayer group has been together for some time and know each other well, including their giftings and weaknesses, and are growing together in a relationship with Jesus Christ, then they are in a position for God to call and equip them for these types of prayer and spiritual warfare assignments.

In PRMI, the cohorts that are most used of God are those in which the members have spent considerable time praying together and forming these deep relationships. Such personal relationships among team members that function within the fellowship of the Father, Son, and Holy Spirit are not incidental to intercession that advances the Kingdom of God, but essential to it.

Lesson # 9 - God Has No Second String

In this entire cast of actors, some of whom have been named in this book from intercessors to senators on the Committee, each had a vital and irreplaceable role in the victory of Brett Kavanaugh being confirmed to the Supreme Court.

What if any one of us had failed to play our role? What if any called to be intercessors had through disobedience, or lack of faith, or fear, or a myriad of other reasons taken ourselves out of the assignments that the Lord had for us? Would the outcome have been different? If we failed to play our role, just as a baseball team has a second string of players ready to take the first-string players' place on the field if need be, did God have a second string of intercessors ready and waiting to take our place?

Chapter 11 Summary of Timeless Lessons for Prayer Warriors

After a major prayer battle, my mentor in the work of intercession, Archer Torrey, said, "When it comes to the work of the Kingdom that the Lord has called you to, there is no second string!"

This gets very personal for all of us! What if, on that rainy morning of September 27 as I was enjoying teaching on evangelism, I had refused the Lord's invitation to leave the group and head up the mountain where I was to be caught up in the heavenlies in a struggle with high-level demons? Was there a second string of intercessors ready to go up the mountain in my place to fight that battle? Or what if I had been afraid of provoking controversy and not sent out the invitation to intercessors to be 100% committed and prepared for commanding Satan's kingdom to be divided? Or, was I the only one prepared at that particular place and time to obey the specific command that the Lord was giving to provide a strategic part in His vast battle plan? I believe this to be the case. There is no second string! If I had not obeyed, then I would not have provided the Holy Spirit empowered words and actions to accomplish His intended objectives in those skirmishes with high-level demons.

Is this not true for every one called into this prayer battle? In the Lord's master battle strategy, each had a vital role to play. We were each part of a vast concert of prayer that was defeating Satan and advancing God's Kingdom plans on earth. If any one of us who were called by our Commander Jesus Christ into these engagements had stepped out of the battle or failed to fulfill our assignment, no second string was waiting to take our place. Then the outcome would have been different. Satan's schemes would have prevailed and Judge Kavanaugh may not have been confirmed to the US Supreme Court.

By insisting that every one of us has a role in the concert of prayer, and by virtue of our unique personality, calling, and location in the battle being irreplaceable, I must add a caveat. The larger group of intercessors who back up the leadership are likely more easily replaced with a second string. One or more could quit, and another one or more could be added. It is like the pyramid of an army. At the base, the removal of a few foot soldiers causes less damage than the removal of its generals or commanders.

It is the same in the Lord's prayer army. God has raised up leaders to embody a prayer movement and to grow a team of intercessors around them. If the leader is removed early on, the prayer endeavor can be halted. If the prayer group, cohort, or movement is well established and there are others who are well equipped, then the mantle of anointed leadership may be passed on to another. However, many times, once a prayer leader is removed, the movement collapses. There is a timeless lesson and warning in this. Each intercessor in God's prayer army plays a critical and irreplaceable role in the midst of the battle. At the same time, we must work with the Holy Spirit to equip and mentor those whom the Lord is raising up to replace us when we are either called out or taken out of the battle.

The Rev. Archer Torrey, founder of Jesus Abbey in South Korea, mentored me as an intercessor, often through example, by taking me with him into the engagements and by spending time teaching me through after-action reviews. He also prayed for me to be anointed with the Holy Spirit. Then, after leading a worship service, he tripped and fell, hit his head on a rock, went into a coma for six weeks, and died. The mantle of leadership he embodied in the movement of the Holy Spirit was then passed on to those he had personally mentored—his son Ben, nephew Peyton, and me. (There were also many others, but these are the three that I know the most about.) We are the second string who stepped into the first string on different aspects of this great movement of the Holy Spirit.

But what of the sovereignty of God? As we look to future battles for the soul of America, will not God accomplish His purposes in spite of us? The timeless lesson we learn from this battle is a mystery and a paradox. God is sovereign, and He will work out His purposes. But in the mystery of His grace, He has chosen to give us momentous responsibility to join Him as coworkers and friends, whether on the mountain as intercessors or in the melee of politics, to cooperate with the Holy Spirit in defeating Satan's schemes and advancing the Kingdom of Jesus Christ on earth. It remains a mystery what God would have done had we not fulfilled the roles He had called us to. No doubt the Lord had other plans, and no doubt ultimately His will would have prevailed. Yet, if the Father in His sovereign governance of the world includes us, His born-again friends and coworkers into His purposes, then our faith and obedience really do matter. Then perhaps God's intended course of action in a specific situation could forever be lost by our disobedience. That is the mystery and the burden of being an intercessor.

The work of prayer is crucial in the battle of preserving America as a nation founded on Judeo-Christian values. If America is to continue to be both a bulwark against Satan's plans of imposing godlessness, and remain a nation that provides freedom and prosperity for those of biblical faith to have the human means to take part in the global advancement of the Kingdom of God, we must remain a people of prayer.

With these timeless lessons learned, let us turn toward the future before us.

In the closing chapter we will present three on-site participants in this battle: Judge Kavanaugh, Senator Lindsey Graham (Republican Senator from South Carolina) and the young journalist intern Jon Brown. They each spoke words discerning the nature of the battle we have been through, and offer prophetic insight into what may be ahead in the battle for the soul of America.

12

Three Prophetic Words for the Battle for America

Three people spoke prophetic words during this confirmation battle. Through their words the Lord exposed the true nature of the battle we had just been through, providing us with guidance for the character of future battles we will face and the work of prayer and spiritual warfare ahead. I believe their words were spoken, if not by the direct inspiration of the Holy Spirit, then certainly with deep insight, being consistent with all we have experienced during spiritual battles. Each of the three men, in their own unique way, worked in accordance with God's plan to defeat Satan's schemes and advance God's Kingdom purposes.

I feel I should let them speak for themselves in their own words without a lot of commentary. Please listen to them and ask the Lord to show you what is from Him and what may be guidance for the battles that will take place.

The First Prophetic Word Given by Brett Kavanaugh

It was the man at the center of the entire battle whom I believe gave a prophetic word of warning about the possible long-term consequences of what was done to him and the nation. In his opening statement of response to the allegations of Dr. Ford and to the cascade of last-minute accusations of sexual misconduct, Judge Kavanaugh said these words to the senators on the Judiciary Committee.

(You really need to watch this to get the flavor and the passion with which it was spoken). (https://youtu.be/IL94tAsjYfk)

Transcript from the NY Times:[117] (I have selected the portions in which Kavanaugh describes what happened to him and his family, and the tactics deployed by the Democrats and the Left.)

...The day after the allegation appeared, I told this committee that I wanted a hearing as soon as possible to clear my name. I demanded a hearing for the very next day. Unfortunately, it took the committee 10 days to get to this hearing. In those 10 long days, as was predictable and as I predicted, my family and my name have been totally and permanently destroyed by vicious and false additional accusations. The 10-day delay has been harmful to me and my family, to the Supreme Court and to the country. When this allegation first arose, I welcomed any kind of investigation. Senate, F.B.I. or otherwise. The committee now has conducted a thorough investigation, and I've cooperated fully...

...This confirmation process has become a national disgrace. The Constitution gives the Senate an important role in the confirmation process. But you have replaced "advice and consent" with "search and destroy." Since my nomination in July, there's been a frenzy on the left to come up with something, anything to block my confirmation. Shortly after I

---

[117] https://www.nytimes.com/2018/09/26/us/politics/read-brett-kavanaughs-complete-opening-statement.html?partner=rss&emc=rss

was nominated, the Democratic Senate leader said he would "oppose me with everything he's got." A Democratic senator on this committee publicly referred to me as evil. Evil. Think about that word. And said that those that supported me were "complicit and evil." Another Democratic senator on this committee said, "Judge Kavanaugh is your worst nightmare." A former head of the Democratic National Committee said, "Judge Kavanaugh will threaten the lives of millions of Americans for decades to come."

I understand the passions of the moment. But I would say to those senators: Your words have meaning. Millions of Americans listened carefully to you. Given comments like those, is it any surprise that people have been willing to do anything, to make any physical threat against my family? To send any violent email to my wife, to make any kind of allegation against me, and against my friends, to blow me up and take me down.

You sowed the wind for decades to come. I fear that the whole country will reap the whirlwinds.

The behavior of several of the Democratic members of this committee at my hearing a few weeks ago was an embarrassment. But at least it was just a good old-fashioned attempt at Borking. Those efforts didn't work. When I did at least O.K. enough at the hearings that it looks like I might actually get confirmed, a new tactic was needed. Some of you were lying in wait and had it ready. This first allegation was held in secret for weeks by a Democratic member of this committee and by staff. It would be needed only if you couldn't take me out on the merits. When it was needed, this allegation was unleashed and publicly deployed over Dr. Ford's wishes.

And then, and then, as no doubt was expected, if not planned, came a long series of false last-minute smears designed to scare me and drive me out of the process before any hearing occurred. Crazy stuff. Gangs, illegitimate children, fights on boats in Rhode Island. All nonsense. Reported breathlessly and often uncritically by the media. This has destroyed my family and my good name. A good name built up through decades of very hard work and public service at the highest levels of the American government.

This whole two-week effort has been a calculated and orchestrated political hit, fueled with apparent pent-up anger about President Trump and the 2016 election, fear that has been unfairly stoked about my judicial record, revenge on behalf of the Clintons, and millions of dollars in money from outside left-wing opposition groups.

This is a circus. The consequences will extend long past my nomination. The consequences will be with us for decades. This grotesque and coordinated character assassination will dissuade confident and good people of all political persuasions from serving our country. And as we all know in the United States political system of the early 2000s, what goes around comes around.

I am an optimistic guy. I always try to be on the sunrise side of the mountain, to be optimistic about the day that is coming, but today, I have to say that I fear for the future.

Last time I was here, I told this committee that a federal judge must be independent, not swayed by public or political pressure. I said I was such a judge. And I am.

I will not be intimidated into withdrawing from this process. You have tried hard. You've given it your all. No one can question your efforts. Your coordinated and well-funded efforts to destroy my good name and destroy my family will not drag me out. The vile threats of violence against my family will not drive me out. You may defeat me in the final vote, but you'll never get me to quit. Never....

There is, of course, a lot more Judge Kavanaugh said to powerfully defend his name. It is important to hear his words about America reaping the whirlwind of what Democrats, in collusion with the Radical Left, have done. Especially note the twisting of what is good and evil, and the dire consequences of that twisting with his words: *"You sowed the wind. For decades to come,*

I fear the whole country will reap the whirlwind."[118]

The Second Prophetic Word given by Senator Lindsey Graham (R) from South Carolina

Watch the video to hear the fire in his words. You also need to see this in order to watch his interaction with Kavanaugh and the Democratic senators on the Judiciary Committee.[119] This was on September 27th toward the end of the hearings. I believe this is a prophetic word that cut right through the fog and confusion and named the evil that was being perpetuated by the Democrats.

Sen. Lindsey Graham: Are you aware that at 9:23 pm on the night of July the 9th, the day you were nominated to the Supreme Court by President Trump, Sen. [Chuck] Schumer [D-NY] said 23 minutes after your nomination, "I'll oppose Judge Kavanaugh's nomination with everything. I hope a bipartisan majority will do the same. The stakes are simply too high for anything less." If you weren't aware of it, you are now.

Did you meet with Sen. Dianne Feinstein [D-CA] on August 20?

Brett Kavanaugh: I did meet with Sen. Feinstein.

Graham: Did you know that her staff had already recommended a lawyer to Dr. Ford?

Kavanaugh: I did not know that.

Graham: Did you know that her and her staff had these allegations for over 20 days?

Kavanaugh: I did not know that at the time.

Graham: If you wanted an FBI investigation, you could have come to us. What you [Democrats] want to do is destroy this guy's life, "hold this seat open and hope you win in 2020." You've said

---

[118] https://canadafreepress.com/article/a-looming-sense-of-foreboding-in-america

[119] https://www.usatoday.com/videos/news/politics/2018/09/27/sen-graham-kavanaugh-this-not-job-interview-hell/1449194002/

that. Not me.

You got nothing to apologize for. When [you see Justices] Sotomayer and Kagan, say hello because I voted for them.

[To the Democrats] I'd never do to them what you've done to this guy. This is the most unethical sham since I've been in politics and if you really wanted to know the truth, you sure as hell wouldn't have done what you've done to this guy.

Are you a gang rapist?

Kavanaugh: No.

Graham: I cannot imagine what you and your family have gone through. Boy, you [Democrats] all want power. God, I hope you never get it. I hope the American people can see through this sham. That you knew about it and you held it. You had no intention of protecting Dr. Ford. None.

She's as much of a victim as you are. God, I hate to say it because these have been my friends, but let me tell you, when it comes to this, you're looking for a fair process, you came to the wrong town at the wrong time, my friend. Do you consider this a job interview?

Kavanaugh: The advice and consent rule is like —

Graham: Do you consider that you've been through a job interview?

Kavanaugh: I've been through a process of advice and consent under the Constitution which —

Graham: Would you say you've been through hell?

Kavanaugh: I've been through hell and then some.

Graham: This is not a job interview.

Kavanaugh: Yeah.

Graham: This is hell. This is going to destroy the ability of good people to come forward because of this crap. Your high school yearbook.

You have interacted with professional women all your life, not one accusation. You're supposed to be Bill Cosby when you're a junior and senior in high school. And all of a sudden you got over it. It's been my understanding that if you drug women and rape them for two years in high school, you probably don't stop.

Here's my understanding. If you lived a good life, people would recognize it like the American bar association has the gold standard. "His integrity is absolutely unquestioned. He is the very circumspect in his personal conduct, harbors no biases or prejudices. Entirely ethical. Is a really decent person. Is warm, friendly, unassuming. He's the nicest person." ...

One thing I can say you should be proud of: Ashley, you should be proud of this. That you raised a daughter who had the good character to pray for Dr. Ford. To my Republican colleagues, if you vote no, you're legitimizing the most despicable thing I have seen in my time in politics. ...

[To Democrats: Do you want this seat? I hope you never get it!][120]

I hope you're on the Supreme Court. That's exactly where you should be. And I hope that the American people will see through this charade. And I wish you well. You well. And I intend to vote for you, and I hope everybody who's fair minded will.

The Third Prophetic Word Given by Jon Brown

This final word is from my young journalist friend, Jon Brown. He has been mentioned a number of times in this book as a source of information and insight about what was taking place during the confirmation process. Jon discerned the ominous spiritual currents at work in our nation that erupted in the Kavanaugh confirmation process. He prophetically named what may be ahead unless stopped by intercessory prayer and wise political leadership.

He wrote an essay for the Daily Caller entitled: OPINION: TO BE A DAILY CALLER INTERN IN DC DURING THE TRUMP ERA 1:30 PM 12/29/2018 | Jon Brown | Associate Editor[121]   Excerpts from his

---

[120]Not in the transcript, but in the video: https://www.youtube.com /watch?v=5Nzg5Bf__V4 --

[121]https://dailycaller.com/2018/12/29/daily-caller-intern-trump-era/

article:

"Reflecting on an unforgettable season of chaos and history, I am sobered by some of what I saw. Space allows only for what was my most memorable experience…My first day in the newsroom coincided with the first day of Judge Brett Kavanaugh's appearance before the Senate Judiciary Committee. Therefore, I took an unusually personal interest in following what became a national spectacle. What began as cordial, somewhat boring congressional hearings soon darkened into yet another black cloud in the gathering cultural storm."

"…on Oct. 6, the day of Kavanaugh's Senate confirmation vote, I threw on my suit, walked down from my house to Capitol Hill and decided to find out. I wanted to watch with my own eyes the conclusion to this national ordeal. To my surprise, the police let me right in after a brief screening. I felt entirely out of place as I wandered into the sprawling Capitol, which somehow manages to seem vast and small at the same time. My hurried footsteps echoed off the ornate, vaulted hallways as I looked for some way into the Senate press gallery. At length, I discovered that the gallery had been shut because of protesters disrupting the vote."

"Disappointed, I returned outside and huddled with other media beside the Senate steps. One by one, senators emerged and shuffled off to their chauffeurs. Opposite where I was, protesters had gathered to await the arrival of Vice President Mike Pence to his motorcade. As he descended the steps with a defiantly friendly wave, they hissed, booed and screamed at him."

"I then heard cries erupt across the street at the Supreme Court. News had reached the protesters there that Kavanaugh had been confirmed. I made my way over in time to see them storm the steps. They banged and clawed at the Court's 12-ton bronze doors, which depict key scenes from 3,000 years of Western legal history. "Shut it down!" they yelled. The unintentional symbolism struck me."

"They wept and wailed in desperation until dusk when the Capitol Police at last dispersed them."

"Watching them on television or social media from a distance, it might be easy to dehumanize these protesters. Their hysterical behavior has been mocked by many. But as I slipped silently among them, reading their hand-written signs and looking into their eyes, I felt sympathy. Many were genuine victims of sexual assault and abuse. Others had some other pain which had been co-opted, distilled and channeled by shrewd organizers."

Protesters bang on the doors of the U.S. Supreme Court after storming the steps as Brett Kavanaugh is sworn in as an Associate Justice of the court in Washington, U.S., October 6, 2018. (Photo by REUTERS/James Lawler Duggan)

"Their targets that day were Donald Trump, Mike Pence and Brett Kavanaugh, as well as any senator who voted for him. Tomorrow it will be someone else. Some will not rest until the entire system of authority is pulled down. If this politically weaponized pain is to remain a permanent feature of our fracturing institutions, then perhaps weeping and wailing is the only appropriate response."

"The night of Friday's government shutdown was my last in Washington before returning to North Carolina for Christmas. I decided to walk to my house from work, a trip that takes me along the Mall and past all the grand temples which have been raised to American ideals. They seem increasingly to reflect a glory that has departed. Walking around the Capitol, I noticed that the beacon above the dome was lit. This symbol of democracy lighting the world seemed painfully ironic, indicating as it did that Congress was in session well into the night, trying in vain to avert yet another gridlocked failure."

"The evening had an eerie, ominous feel. The moon was full, the weather unseasonably warm and rain fell in fits and starts. Every flag I passed remained at half-staff for former President George Bush, himself a symbol of bygone civility. There was a heavy sense of looming crisis."

"I made my way past the Supreme Court. I paused at the steps and looked up at its doors, remembering those who pounded on them months ago. I thought of the friends I know and care about who would gladly have joined them. I can no longer speak with many of them about the most important things. We talk past each other, our worldviews almost hopelessly incompatible."

"I am seized by what can only be described as grief. I wonder if it is similar to what Americans must have felt in the years before the Civil War when differences became irreconcilable, the middle ground fell away and people began to line up on opposite sides. For now, the battle is mostly spiritual. But for a nation whose people have less and less in common, it is questionable how long that will be so."

"To those at his hearing who were willing to tear it all down to destroy him and maintain power, Kavanaugh paraphrased the prophet Hosea. "You sowed the wind," he warned. "For decades to come, I fear that the whole country will reap the whirlwind." He may have been speaking more prophetically than he knew."

Summary Conclusions: The Battle Before Us

I believe this entire confirmation process has been a revelatory event. Three prophetic and prescient words, one from an outside observer and journalist (Jon Brown) and two from people who were in the vortex of the battle (Judge Kavanaugh and Lindsey Graham). All three expose the terrible evil that we as a nation are facing. They dared to stand up against it and name it. I believe they were able to do so because intercessors were on the mountain, like Moses, Aaron, and Hur, fighting battles in the heavenlies and praying for them as they were doing battle on earth. If their words are to be used by the Holy Spirit to halt and to reverse this trajectory of destruction, that too will be the work of intercessors.

These three voices have presented a vivid picture of what will happen if this evil is not soon stopped. It will be the "whirlwind" of destruction, a calamity to the United States and to humanity.

Let this entire book and these concluding prophetic words call us as intercessors to prepare for future battles that must be fought until these human and demonic foes dedicated to the destruction of America, a nation founded upon Judeo-Christian values and the Greek-born power of reason, are vanquished by the Kingdom of God.

To God be the Glory!

Chapter 12 Three Prophetic Words

Appendix A: Resources to Grow in Intercession and in Spiritual Warfare

Presbyterian-Reformed Ministries International

PRMI was founded in 1966 to pray and work for the spiritual renewal of Presbyterian and Reformed churches. Over the past 50 years, we have grown to include parts of the Body of Christ in many nations, and continue to have a distinctive role in the world wide movement of the Holy Spirit advancing the Gospel of Jesus Christ for the fulfillment of the Great Commission.

www.prmi.org

Presbyterian-Reformed Ministries offers the following opportunities to grow in the work of intercessory prayer and spiritual warfare that is illustrated in the book *Timeless Lessons for Prayer Warriors: Confirming Kavanaugh.* We also provide the way that intercessors may be connected into networks to take part in various prayer initiatives.

Discerning the Times

Receive **Discerning The Times**, an email digest of blogs written by Dr. Zeb Bradford Long offering discernment on current events and educating people to issues that face the Church today for the purpose of mobilizing intercessors.

www.discernwith.us

Other books available by this author related to mobilizing prayer

Prayer that Shapes the Future: How to Pray with Power and Authority

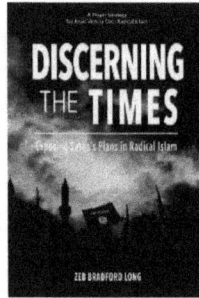

Discerning the Times: Exposing Satan's Plans in Radical Islam

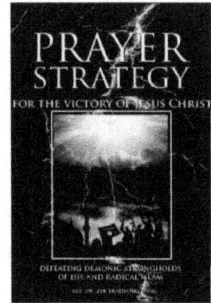

Prayer Strategy For the Victory of Jesus Christ : Defeating Demonic Strongholds of ISIS and Radical Islam

the Dunamis project

"But you will receive power when the Holy Spirit has come upon you, and you will be my witnesses in Jerusalem, and in all Judea and Samaria, and to the farthest parts of the earth." Acts 1:8

Learn how to cooperate with the Holy Spirit to be a witness to Jesus Christ by effectively engaging in ministries of prayer, healing, spiritual warfare, and evangelism for growing the Church and advancing the Kingdom of God.

Dunamis can help you deepen your walk with the Lord and prepare you for effective ministry wherever the Lord has called you. "Dunamis" is the Greek term for "power."

With the Dunamis teaching, you'll discover

- **Solid biblical theology about the person and work of the Holy Spirit in the life of the believer.**
- **Teaching forged from the Scriptures, proven in ministry, and informed by 200 years of renewal and revival movements.**
- **Your spiritual gifts and how to use them effectively in the Kingdom of God.**
- **How to recognize God's guidance for ministry in a given moment through the experience-based lab times and review debriefings.**

The Dunamis Project consists of six units each taught over five days six months apart in the same location. Each event consists of intensive biblical teaching and practical application in the context of prayer and worship. These events are designed to enable every believer to grow in their faith, personal relationship with God, and participation in the ministry of the Holy Spirit.

For more information, go to www.prmi.org

Equipping projects are offered in English, Spanish, Korean, Japanese, Chinese, and other languages in the United States, Central and South America, Canada, the United Kingdom, South Korea, and other locations.

www.ingramcontent.com/pod-product-compliance
Lightning Source LLC
Chambersburg PA
CBHW051825040426
42447CB00006B/367